The Grasshopper Book

The Grasshopper Book

by Wilfrid S. Bronson

ILLUSTRATED BY THE AUTHOR

SUNSTONE PRESS

SANTA FE

Sunstone books may be purchased for educational, business, or sales promotional use. For information please write: Special Markets Department, Sunstone Press, P.O. Box 2321, Santa Fe, New Mexico 87504-2321.

Library of Congress Cataloging-in-Publication Data

Bronson, Wilfrid S. (Wilfrid Swancourt), 1894-
  The grasshopper book / written and illustrated by Wilfrid Swancourt Bronson. --
Large print ed.
    p. cm.
  Originally published: New York : Harcourt, Brace and Company, 1943.
  ISBN 978-0-86534-690-1 (softcover : alk. paper)
  1. Grasshoppers--Juvenile literature. I. Title.
  QL508.A2B73 2008
  595.7'26--dc22

                    2008031551

Published in

WWW.SUNSTONEPRESS.COM
SUNSTONE PRESS / POST OFFICE BOX 2321 / SANTA FE, NM 87504-2321 /USA
(505) 988-4418 / ORDERS ONLY (800) 243-5644 / FAX (505) 988-1025

CONTENTS

1

AESOP DIDN'T KNOW

WHEN I was a boy in Illinois, I used to run for miles across the windswept prairie. Before my flying feet the frightened grasshoppers shot away like popping corn in all directions. Sometimes, in its panic, one would jump right into my open blouse. Often I did not know that this had happened till, unable to find its way out, the frightened insect would begin to bite me. At the same time it would spit "tobacco juice." That was what we called it. But the brown and sticky liquid was actually

3

an acid from the grasshopper's crop, which poured into the bite making it smart and sting severely.

One could hardly blame the creature for using the only way it knew for getting out of its predicament. And in spite of the many bites they gave me I always liked grasshoppers. They do such clownish things so solemnly. For all their sober faces they are so full of the fun of living. It always seemed to me that Aesop's ancient fable, which told how noble is the ant and how worthless is the grasshopper, was somehow most unfair.

You know the story: the ant worked hard all summer saving food for winter, while the grasshopper played and fiddled the happy hours away, and had to go begging to the ant when cold weather came, and died because the ant would not give to the undeserving fellow. But there were a lot of things that Aesop and the people of his time didn't know about natural history.

Even Aesop must have believed in at least one grasshopper which not only survived a winter but lived on forever. Didn't Eos, Greek goddess of the dawn, turn her human husband, Tithonus, into a grasshopper and feed him on nectar and ambrosia so that he would never die? That shows how little they knew about insects. For nectar is a food for ants. Poor Tithonus would have been better off with plenty of spinach.

AESOP DIDN'T KNOW

As a boy I didn't really know just why I felt that Aesop's fable was unfair. But now I do. Whoever studies insects soon finds out that, though many kinds of ants work hard, other kinds are thieves, slave-

makers, murderers, and cannibals, and do no work at all. Then, if he looks up the grasshopper's list of relatives, he discovers that it also has both good and bad, like everybody else.

Hard work is well worth while, of course. But music is important too. No ant can fiddle, but a grasshopper can. And its cousins, the katydids and crickets, are the most talented of insect music makers. There are some odd relations, peculiar but harmless, the walking-sticks and walking-leaves, for example. And there is that terrible branch of the family tree, the praying mantises, which eat other insects alive, including each other.

Also we at least must mention the earwigs who, modern scientists now agree, are relatives of grasshoppers. That some scientists thought otherwise for a long time is easy to understand, since these insects are so much like beetles. Even now no one seems to know the purpose, if any, of the mighty pincers on the little earwigs' bodies. For centuries it was believed by many that these creatures crawled into people's ears and injured them. The one thing that was "known" about earwigs simply wasn't so.

Many people are acquainted with still another group of the grasshopper's relations, especially if they live in cities. They know and cordially detest cockroaches. And lastly, though most of us would never dream that they are even a grasshopper's long lost cousins, there are those other insects which sometimes get into our homes and do great damage: those undercover workers, those silent saboteurs, the termites.

If the roaches and the termites would stay out of our

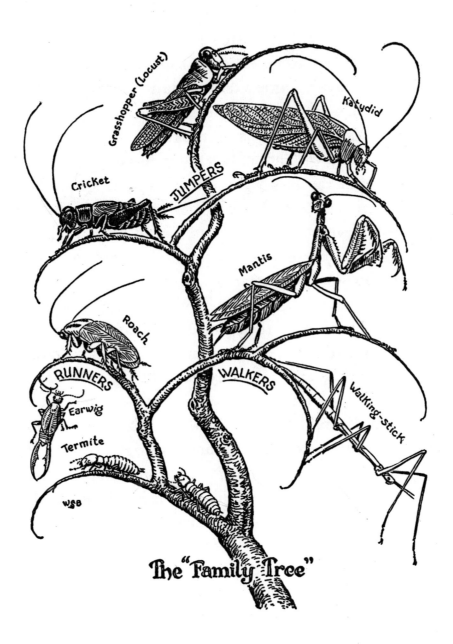

Grasshopper (Locust)

Katydid

Cricket

JUMPERS

Mantis

Roach

RUNNERS

WALKERS

Walking-stick

Earwig

Termite

WSB

The "Family Tree"

houses, we would not dislike them so. Indeed we might admire the termites even more than we do the ants. For in some ways the great termite nations are more marvelous than nations of the ants. Termites had great insect cities with millions of workers, various kinds of soldiers, and with not only a queen but a king as well, ages before the ants began their wondrous works. Termites are related from away back to the roaches which were scurrying about the world for quite a few million years before there were any people for them to bother. And roaches being related also to the grasshoppers, those never-working ne'er-do-wells can claim hard-working termites as their true, if very distant, kin.

But actually the grasshopper is no more a ne'er-do-well than the ant; it simply does the things it has to for a happy and successful life, as any creature so equipped would have to do them. The ant must do quite otherwise or be a failure. The one insect is not really better than the other, only differently designed with different needs and different methods of supplying them. All creatures do the best they can with whatever they may have to do it with. Each thing to its proper uses. We wouldn't try to use a plane to pull a plow, nor try to fly in a tractor. Neither should the grasshopper be expected to live like the ant.

8

Let us consider the ant for a moment, as King Solomon advised, and see if we can be wise about it. We shall understand that ants are equipped to do great things as long as they have each other to depend upon. The queen depends on the workers and soldiers to care for and protect the nation. And they depend on her to produce the eggs from which will hatch the young they will raise to take the place of the ants that die. Thus the nation lives for years and years, and every year sends out young queens to start new nations far and wide. It is wonderful to watch, but of no special credit to the ants. It is just the way, the only way, they are equipped to live. Let a queen die and her entire nation is soon done for.

Now consider the grasshopper. It takes life as it comes, neither building a city nor even any shelter for itself alone. The ant, if unable to find the way home, becomes frantic with fear, since alone its life is meaningless and soon may end. But the grasshopper is at home wherever it happens to be, out in the grassy jungles. At night it sleeps down deep in the tangle, and any tall grass stem may become its tower to climb for enjoyment of the rising sun.

True, on really chilly nights or rainy days it takes little comfort, whereas the ant enjoys a well-earned rest down in its dry and cozy caverns. But the grass-hopper has no liking for a life in such close quarters. Only wide open spaces suit its temperament. It prefers the stored heat in a stone, where it can cling when the sun has set, to the worthy but worrisome housekeeping of the ant.

It lays up no stores of food, as does the ant. Such a thing it is not designed to do. For its brain and body are fashioned for a different style of living. Grown grasshoppers never work over nor worry about their young ones, nor fight in their defense as ants will do. Even so, a female grasshopper makes as sure as possi-ble, for a creature of her kind, that there will always be more like her in the world. And her method must work fairly well. For there are billions and billions of grasshoppers of various kinds today, just as there were when Aesop told his unfair tale more than two thou-sand years ago.

The female grasshopper is furnished with an effi-cient instrument, an egg-placer, and knows exactly how to use it. With it she can hide her eggs beneath the ground. This is the only responsibility life puts upon her. But she does this one great duty very faith-fully. Where she leaves them, the eggs will have a fair chance of escaping harm. She will not live to see it, but after lying out of sight all winter, the eggs will hatch in spring. The baby grasshoppers will not need a nurse's help like infant ants. They will be born ready to feed themselves and hop for their lives whenever necessary.

We admire the ant for working hard and being thrifty. Why not admire the grasshopper for being independent and self-reliant? The main task of both is to keep their kind from perishing from the earth, as it is with all creatures, including ourselves. When wars come, we are willing to give up everything, including our very lives, to save our nation from destruction by the enemy. Men, ants, and grasshoppers preserve their kind, each in his own special way. Since each succeeds age after age, why should one be praised more than the other?

I have written a book about the ants and their truly wonderful ways. It seems only fair to write another one about grasshoppers and their remarkable relatives. So here we are—and first let's have a look at a grasshopper's special equipment. Let's see what makes it so able to live with hardly a worry from its first spring hatching day to its life's end in the fall.

2

A GRASSHOPPER'S MACHINERY

OF ALL living creatures, excepting crabs and lobsters and the like, insects look most like machines. No doubt this is because they have the harder material of their bodies on the outside. Just as the knights of old looked like mechanical men, the insects in their own jointed armor look mechanical. Plainly we see where they are joined, one portion to another, like the parts of an assembled engine.

If hair covers up the joints, as on the body of a bumblebee, much of this machine-like look is lost. It is the insects with the hard smooth surfaces that remind us most of little models of machinery. Seen from the outside, a grasshopper may make us think of several different mechanisms. And on the inside it will make us think of several more. As a matter of fact, many of our inventions have been in use among the insects for thousands, even millions, of years.

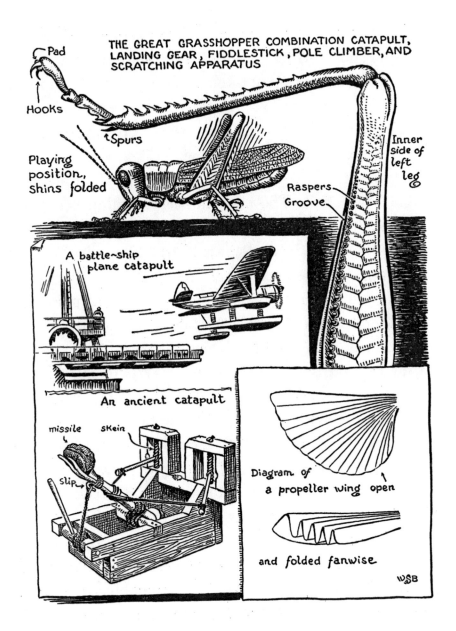

THE GREAT GRASSHOPPER COMBINATION CATAPULT, LANDING GEAR, FIDDLESTICK, POLE CLIMBER, AND SCRATCHING APPARATUS

Pad

Hooks

Spurs

Playing position, Shins folded

Inner side of left leg

Raspers

Groove

A battle-ship plane catapult

An ancient catapult

missile

skein

slip

Diagram of a propeller wing open

and folded fanwise

WSB

In days of old soldiers used a mechanism called a catapult for hurling heavy rocks upon the enemy. It was worked with stout skeins of sinew or of elastic horsehair very tightly twisted which, when suddenly released, untwisted with great force, casting missiles far too heavy for men to throw. Today we use catapults, worked by compressed air, to launch scout planes from battleships. The most noticeable thing about a grasshopper is its great hind legs, its portable living catapults. When it jumps, it is itself the missile. When it jumps and flies it is itself the plane. In place of skeins or air compression, the many powerful muscles in its thighs, arranged almost as though in braids, work a grasshopper's catapults. They pull with the snap of a rat trap on the stiff strong shins. Where shins join feet, big barbs dig into the ground like the spikes of a sprinter, preventing any slip on the take-off.

Once in the air, with the stiffer upper pair of wings spread out straight, a grasshopper becomes a plane indeed. The more delicate lower pair, whirring audibly, are the propellers, one on either side of the fuselage, the grasshopper's body. Some kinds of grasshoppers suddenly produce a loud crackling sound while flying, like a plane having engine trouble. But they seem able to crackle or not, just as they please, though how or why they do it nobody knows. Sometimes they seem to do it so that other grasshoppers of their kind may follow them. They might turn it on to startle a pursuing bird. Or maybe they simply like to make a noise. Possibly the crackling only happens unintentionally when the grasshopper's propeller wings are raised a little too high and strike against the plane wings.

As soon as it makes a landing, the lower wings fold up in pleats, like fans, along its sides, and the upper wings are laid back over them as covers. As the insect alights, its catapults become a part of its landing gear. And at any moment those most accomplished long hind legs may be used as fiddlesticks. The coarse outer wings are the fiddles, which a grasshopper can play one at a time, in solo, or together in a sort of duet with itself. The shin is folded into a groove on the underside of the thigh to get it out of the way, when music, not jumping, is in order.

Not that much music is produced as far as human hearers are concerned; just a series of dainty rasps such as is made by the winding of a very small watch or by drawing the points of a small comb lightly across the handle of the brush. The sound is audible to our ears for only a few feet, and the grasshopper makes it by rubbing a row of tiny points, on the inside of its thigh, across a hard ridge on the wing. Perhaps the grasshopper itself hears and enjoys overtones too subtle for our ears, but this scraping is all the fiddling it can do.

Only the males are provided with these so-called fiddle-and-bow arrangements on wings and legs. And perhaps the grasshoppers themselves would readily agree with us that they really don't make music. They do not appear to consider the sound they make as anything more than a signal system for saying a few simple things to others of their kind. A male may come close to another male and make a single "zzzzt" with one hind leg. It may get the same in return. Since this shows that each recognizes the other's existence, it may be taken to mean "Hello" and "Hello yourself," but that's about all. When a male approaches a female with a goodly number of "zzzzts," he can be considered to be saying, "I am charmed and hope you like me too."

When the female hears this, having a sort of eardrum on each side of her body, just as he does, but lacking fiddle and bow, she cannot answer in "zzzzts." Her actions speak. If she doesn't walk away or jump beyond his sight, she probably does not dislike him. His rasping signals seem to be the only sounds that interest her. She may be able to hear other sounds, but it is doubtful if she listens to them.

At this moment a male cricket in one of my insect cages is playing his own type of fiddle so loudly and continuously that the study seems saturated with the shrill vibrations. He is standing within one half inch of a female grasshopper's ears, yet she is not disturbed, not even vaguely interested. She goes on munching an apple paring as though he didn't exist. Only now, when he swings around and almost touches her face with his, does she pay the least attention to him. Not because his noise annoys but because he is standing on her breakfast, she reaches up with one front foot and pushes his inquisitive face away.

Besides fiddling and jumping, there are various other ways in which a grasshopper uses its legs. In spite of their name, some kinds spend a lot of time where there is no grass. Nor do they hop very much, but instead sit still, enjoying the heat of the glaring sun on some flat empty space of ground. Now and then they raise their hind legs, knees slightly bent, above their backs, like birds half stretching their wings. The brilliant sunlight does not blind them though it pours straight into their unclosable eyes. Comfortably they rest, occasionally taking walks.

Once in a while a grasshopper will walk as many as a dozen steps without stopping. But usually it is two steps forward—stop a second—two steps forward—stop a second, and so on. While the long hind legs take one slow step apiece, the four short legs ahead of them do the same. But if the long legs move more rapidly, the shorter legs must each take twice as many steps to hold up their end. For toes each foot has two strong hooks, and for heels small spikes stick into the ground behind the smaller feet, just as bigger spikes do behind the big hind feet.

Added to these two non-skid devices, on the sole of each foot are little pads which are a special aid in climbing. For in each pad are minute hollow hairs which can secrete a sticky stuff to help a grasshopper hold fast to such slippery things as the stems and leaves of grass. With its downward pointing spikes, a grasshopper goes up a grass stem like a repair man ascending a telephone pole with climbing-spurs. But instead of repairing anything, the hungry insect is more likely to do some damage to its pole of grass.

The two front feet are used to hold a grass blade steady while the grasshopper scallops the edges with its sideways-working jaws. These front feet also keep the eyes and feelers clean. To polish the right eye, the right front foot is used, always rubbing from the upper edge of the eye downward, slowly, several times. The left front foot takes care of the other eye, of course.

Feelers are cleaned when the grasshopper is resting on some smooth resisting thing, such as a stone or a stout blade of grass, or, here in the study, on the floor of the cage. It lowers its head, lays a feeler on the floor, places the nearest forefoot on it, and slowly pulls it free. Dust thus removed is cleaned from the foot in the mouth.

If an autumn night has been pretty cold, a sunbathing grasshopper seems to itch all over as it warms up and its blood begins to move more rapidly. I have watched the kind of grasshopper known as Red-leg at such times, and though it may have been only cleaning up it appeared to be scratching too. It rubbed the side of its face on the stone where it sat, then passed a front foot over its face many times. Apparently this only made the itching worse, for it suddenly shot a hind shin, with its bigger barbs, away forward and raked its forehead a half dozen times with lightning speed. It flicked the big shin back along its side, then cleaned it with six or seven snatches of a middle foot, which foot was then washed in its mouth. That grasshopper looked quite uncomfortable, as did several others acting similarly close by.

Though grasshoppers spruce up far less than katydids, they keep their eyes and feelers always very clean. For not only do feelers feel, but those on its forehead probably tell the grasshopper how things smell, while the lesser ones at the corners of its mouth are tasters, touching the food continually as the insect eats. Eyes not only locate food but possible mates, as well as enemies.

When my grandmother wanted to read or peel potatoes, she wore her "nigh-to" glasses. When she wished to watch the carriages go by, she put her "far-offs" on. She had to have two pairs of glasses because her eyes couldn't change from short to long distance looking by themselves.

A grasshopper cannot adjust its eyes either. But instead of having two kinds of spectacles, it has two kinds of eyes: a set of three very small ones for viewing objects within a few inches of its face, and a pair of big ones to watch the world about it to the distance of several yards on every side. The three small eyes, one in front of each big eye and one in the middle of its forehead, are called simple eyes. The two big eyes are called compound, because they are made up, or compounded, of thousands of little eyes.

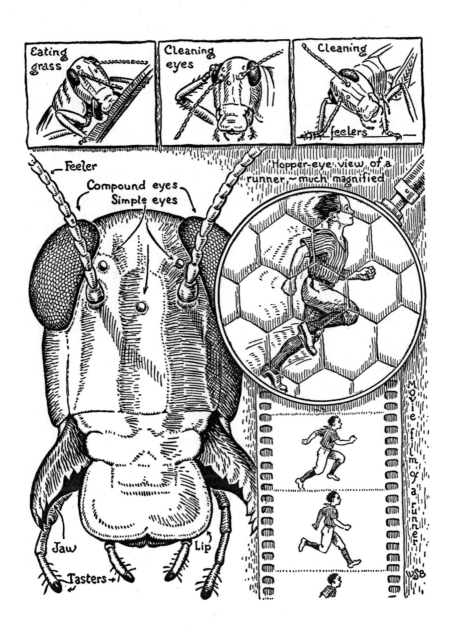

Eating grass

Cleaning eyes

Cleaning feelers

Feeler

Compound eyes
Simple eyes

Hopper-eye view of a runner ~ much magnified

Jaw

Lip

Tasters

Movie film of a runner

Now eyes are natural cameras, cameras which really see the things they focus on. Through their living lenses they are always making pictures in our minds. The simple eyes of the grasshopper could be called the box cameras which make close-up still pictures in its insect mind. The compound eyes make its moving pictures. Because its eyes are not adjustable like ours, the grasshopper needs both box-camera-still-picture-simple eyes, and movie-camera-motion-picture-compound eyes.

The compound eyes cannot be rolled as our eyes can. But the thousands of little eyes in each of them face outward in all directions. Each one makes its own picture of whatever is before it, but all their views are blended into one in the grasshopper's brain, just as thousands of views in a movie film are blended into one moving picture on the screen.

So when a grasshopper spies you walking in the field, it doesn't see several thousand of you, but only one. As each tiny eye's view blends with the others, the insect has a moving picture of you; it sees you coming. And since a grasshopper is designed like the jackrabbit, with big hind legs for quick escape from trouble rather than for self-defense, it jumps just in case you are an enemy. Though it may take some account of your gigantic size, probably it notices very little else besides your movement or the sudden dimming of the light as your shadow falls upon it. To the grasshopper both those things are signs of approaching danger.

But because it can jump so much farther than it can clearly see, there is no use in choosing a direction. Anywhere but toward the possible enemy will do. Most kinds of grasshoppers are hard to spot unless they move, being colored like their surroundings. But few seem to rely much on their good disguises, putting their trust rather in as many all-out jumps as may be needed to get away. Though taking no special aim for the first jump, they never continue in a straight line, always zigzagging, no jump following another in the same direction. If old enough to fly, some zigzag in the air also. This makes them more difficult to catch, in the air or on the ground.

On the other hand, if a grasshopper has not been frightened and is taking its time, it seldom jumps farther than it can see. Rather it appears to choose the direction and to pick a landing place, carefully judging the distance, swaying its head from side to side about as far as the distance between its eyes. Seeing the selected spot from two slightly different points of view should give it a better sense of just how hard to jump to reach it.

Of course the wild haphazard jumping that it does when frightened sometimes carries a grasshopper straight into trouble rather than to safety. It may land, among other places, in a meadow spider's web or in a nearby pond or stream. Though it can swim, the very kicking of its long hind legs will bring any lurking game fish up for dinner. Even if no fish or frog or turtle eats it, a grasshopper may drown, being heavy in the head and having shins so thin that every strong kick slices water, and each drawing up of the legs backs water till the swimmer almost stops. This is even worse with katydids whose legs are even longer in proportion. It is a little better with crickets, but all are pretty poor navigators, tending to list to one side or the other and thus to swim in circles or to sink.

No doubt a grasshopper sinks sooner if water gets through its "portholes." Insects breathe through a row of holes along each side, not through nostrils in their heads. These numerous openings lead into windpipes which do not lead to lungs. Instead they branch into ever smaller tubes which take air to every portion of their bodies, even through the thin tissue of the wings.

All these air tubes plus several air-filled spaces just beneath the shell of its back, make the grasshopper lighter in the air. But if these tubes and spaces fill with water, the grasshopper will drown. The air is pumped in and out by muscles in the abdomen which expands and contracts along two pleats upon the under side. The skin between its armored sections being flexible, the grasshopper thus takes in and expels air like an accordion or bellows.

Air is necessary to purify a creature's blood. We mammals mix air with our blood through the thin membranes of our lungs. But the whole inside of an insect acts like a lung, air passing through the thin walls of the tubes throughout the body. For insects don't have arteries to carry their pale blood. Their entire interior is filled with it like a bottle full of vinegar. The insect's muscles, nerves, and organs—crop, stomach, gizzard, and so on—are surrounded by the blood. The pulsing of the long tubular heart keeps the blood in motion much as you can keep up a circulation in your tub by repeatedly opening and closing your hand beneath the water. Enclosed by its armor and surrounded by its blood, the inner organs of an insect are, in this respect, like the mechanism of an electric ice-box which runs inside a sealed container filled with oil.

The end of a male grasshopper's body is rather rounded, whereas the female's body ends in a point.

Though she has no fiddle, the female grasshopper has a more important instrument all her own, and with it in the fall she does her bit for the great grasshopper race. Seeking a spot where the soil is not too tightly packed, she lays her eggs as deeply underground as her abdomen will reach. On its very tip is the egg-placer composed of four hard movable prongs. At first they are held all close together in a point as she presses them against the earth. As they slowly penetrate, she opens them now and then, packing the soil outward on all sides of the little pit that she is making, without bringing any of it to the surface.

The muscles which move the prongs are very strong. A grasshopper in one of my cages, not satisfied with the dirt I had arranged for her, tried to prepare a place for her eggs by pushing her egg-placer between a big string bean and the wooden floor. Though the bean was four times her size, the prongs lifted it over and over apparently with the utmost ease.

The egg-placer is rather like the expanding reamer used by men in drilling wells. And almost as automatically as a well-drilling machine the grasshopper goes about her task. Though she has never laid any eggs before nor seen other grasshoppers lay them, she performs this most important act of her life with per-

SIMPLIFIED PLAN OF AN INSECT

DIGESTION

HEART

WSB

EXPLANATION

Grey = blood and muscle~

Black = brain and nerves~

White = air tubing

‖‖‖‖‖ = organs~

━━━ = armor~~

Nerves, blood, and air reach
every part and member~~~

fect precision. Just as she inherited a body with an egg-placer on it, she inherited also the impulse and ability to use it.

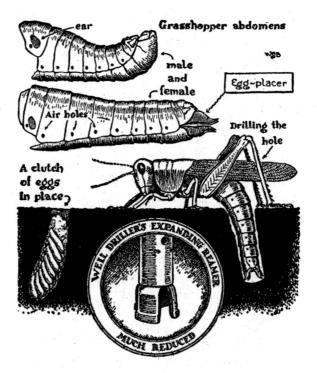

This automatic knowledge is called instinct. It comes without teaching and without the need for thought. Though we humans think, we have our instincts too. We do not think, "I must take my finger from this red-hot stove!" We take it away automatically, instinctively. Just as surely, if more calmly, the grasshopper makes all the moves that go with laying and placing her eggs.

When she can drill no farther she spreads the prongs of her egg-placer once more, and from between them there emerges the first egg. It is pale tan, covered with wet glue, and shaped like a pickle. Gradually raising her abdomen, she lays from two to three dozen eggs in the hole. The performance ends with more liquid glue, which pours down and fills in all about them. This glue is very foamy and, hardening quickly, bubbles and all, it surrounds the eggs with a light and airy stuff which just fits the form of the little pit and is strong enough to keep the sides from caving in upon them.

The laying over with, the grasshopper now leaves the spot. But she hasn't put all her eggs in one "basket." A few days later she may bore and lay in another place, and again somewhere else a few days after that. Surely some will be there still and ready to hatch when spring warms up the ground. Against freezing they need no protection. In fact some kinds of grasshopper eggs, in cool and temperate climates, will not hatch unless first frozen for a while, like the seeds and bulbs of various northern plants. But there are dangers against which the female grasshopper has no means of protecting her eggs. Yet for her to worry about them would be useless since she is not likely to live long after laying, and so could do little more than she does to secure their future.

There is no broodiness about her and she doesn't hover protectively over her eggs. Once laid they are part of her past. Truly they are behind her. She has done all she was designed to do. Though she may linger through frosts and snowstorms in some protecting crevice, and even crawl out during a January thaw, drab and feeble, she can hop but a few rheumatic inches and there is little if anything she can eat. Better to have died soon after laying, for now she rouses in her misery only to perish anyhow. Unlike the ant she was not destined to survive; though the eggs she laid will carry on her kind.

3

A GRASSHOPPER'S GROWTH

LIKE any other eggs, the ones the grasshopper hides within the earth are very nourishing, and various creatures seek them out as food. One of these is the blister beetle which lays about four hundred of its own eggs in the ground where grasshoppers are laying. The beetle grubs soon hatch and each one crawls till it comes to a clutch of grasshopper eggs. Their covering of glue is no defense against its jaws. It creeps right in and settles down to feast upon them for about three weeks. After that it burrows into the ground for the winter, leaving few if any of the eggs unharmed.

The maggots of several kinds of flies also fatten on the same rich fare. And on a nice autumn night, a delighted skunk will dig up all the new-laid grasshopper eggs that he can find. His nose is very keen for finding such a supper. He does an especially good job on a well cut lawn, for here the digging is easy, just as the

laying was. He attacks from above while the burrow-
ing mole helps himself with relish from below. There
may be scores of skunks, hundreds of moles, and thousands of flies and blister beetles in one square mile.
But only one defense is used against them all, the simple device of laying so many eggs that these searching
plunderers miss millions of them.

Finally there comes a fair spring day when the lucky
little grasshoppers hatch. The majority of insects begin
life as caterpillars or maggots or grubs of some sort,
eat furiously for a while, and then sink into a deep
sleep during which all the alterations come about that
change them from infants into adults. Their baby state
is very different from their grown-up state. A caterpil-
lar looks nothing like a butterfly, a maggot isn't like a
fly, a grub bears no resemblance to a beetle or an ant.
But a baby grasshopper is a grasshopper from the start.
Lacking only wings, it is otherwise like its parents,
except, of course, in its proportions. In common with
many other infant animals, it has a head and legs
which look a lot too large for its body. Besides the
droll appearance this creates, it even shares a little of
their look of charming innocence.

When ant babies hatch there are doting nurses to
help them out. Young grasshoppers have to help them-

selves, and what they must do to get a start in life would not appear to be easy. This is what happens.

The egg, which usually stands with the little grasshopper's head end uppermost, splits at the top and about half way down the front. Thus the big eyes are almost the first things uncovered, and this egg-opening is the one and only eye-opening of the insect's life. From its first glance onward it will "look the whole world in the face" unblinkingly. But of course on first emerging from the shell it sees nothing anyway, being still down in the earth. It is clad in a thin, tight, transparent film, its hatching skin. In this protective though cramping covering, it has to struggle up through the glue form which holds all its brothers and sisters, and through the dirt which has settled and caked at the surface of the soil. We could crawl out of a manhole while sewed in a gunnysack with equal ease.

Once out of the hole, it gives a few heaves forward, expanding and contracting two swellings on the back of its neck till the cellophane covering breaks over its head and neck and shrivels down off its body. Having no further use for this garment, it walks irresponsibly away, leaving it where it lies. It has taken its first few steps. But it is equally ready to jump and generally does so, making maybe twenty times its own length on the very first try.

If any of us could achieve a jump in like proportion to our height, we should probably break most of our bones in landing. But though it may tip over at the end of a leap, the little grasshopper picks itself up no worse for a tumble, and ready for a lifetime of leaping, in which one hundred times its own length soon becomes just ordinary jumping.

Jumping for fun, for transportation, and at times for safety's sake; eating for pleasure and to satisfy hunger, the grasshopper grows rapidly. It is ready in about a week to molt, to shed its hard outer covering for a larger size. Within the old armor the entire surface of its body has increased, getting rather rumpled for lack of space, like a soft hat packed in too small a box.

Molting is most likely to occur on a bright and sunny day. The armor opens right along the middle of the back. Then slowly the grasshopper raises its head, gently pulling its feelers free from their old cases. Now it moves forward slightly, lifting out its legs which leave their cases without too much friction, since the barbs on all the shins point downward.

Once the grasshopper is clear, the rumples soon smooth out, giving it greater dimensions all around.

This filling out is aided and perfected by the grasshopper's swallowing as much air as it can. The blood, with less room around the swelling stomach and with more pressure from muscles in the chest, or thorax, is forced into every portion of the body. Thus the expanding creature takes its proper form like a rubber pig that is only perfect when fully blown. Unlike the toy, the insect does not collapse when the pressure ends.

Yet if it tries to walk while still soft and moist, the knees of its big hind legs sway and knock. It can jump only a few inches now and, if it does so, lands with a bad list to one side or the other. So it mostly just sits still for a spell, as though recovering from the shock of an awful accident. The nearby mussed-up molted armor certainly makes things look as though something terrible had taken place. It looks like the wreck of a roadster from which the shaken driver has just emerged, or, because it is colorless and translucent now, like the badly mangled ghost of the grasshopper's former self.

But soon the sun has baked the new hide into as tough a crust as was the old. After this has happened three times at intervals of about one week, depending on how warm the weather is, the grasshopper is about half grown. Now tiny fan-shaped stubs appear upon its back, the promises of wings.

After the fourth molt, not counting the shedding of the hatching skin, its wings are half as long as its abdomen. Then when some six weeks old it has a final change of armor and gets a full-length set of wings. To ensure against any complication in this coming-out party, this graduation exercise, the grasshopper molts head down, holding fast to a grass stem with all six feet, though, strangely enough, with the hind legs doubled under it. It has to pull them out of their sheaths around the sharp corners made by the bended knees. Apparently this presents no problem, so soft and pliable are they within, though it must be done slowly. The entire molt may take a full hour to accomplish.

As soon as it is clear, the grasshopper swings around and faces upward, perhaps climbing onto the cast armor still clinging by its dead claws to the stalk. This position gives the best chance for the soft, wet, rumpled wings to unfold properly.

About once a minute the grasshopper heaves hard, contracting its thorax, forcing blood into the wings and air through the network of tiny tubes spreading throughout, unfurling them as we inflate cloth water-wings.

Once completely expanded, the wings begin to dry

36

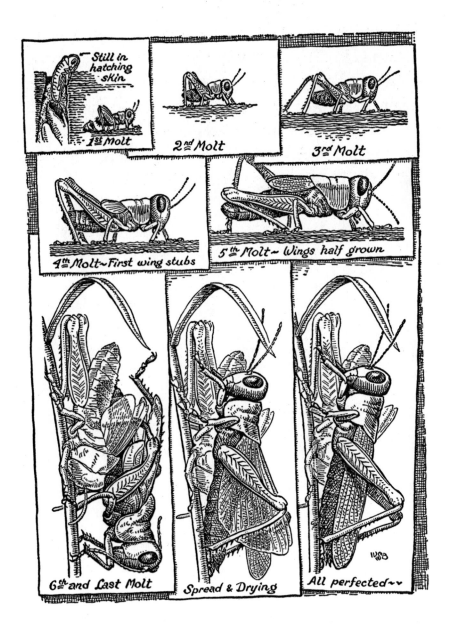

and stiffen and shrink to the thinness necessary for their use in flight. The upper and lower surfaces draw closer and closer together till, between them, they plainly show the contour of the air tubes which, in the stiffening, become wing braces also. All at last is ready for the first flight over the field. The flying machine is finished. The grasshopper is all grown up.

4

GRASSHOPPER PLAGUES

NOT every kind of grasshopper can fly. Some have long wings, some short, some very short, and one kind grows up without acquiring any wings at all. It lives in thickets mostly, where wings would be a useless bother. Their absence, however, makes it mute, a fiddler with no instrument. But out in the open fields, especially on the wide plains and western prairies, grasshoppers can make full use of wings. There millions of them, having eaten all vegetation on their hatching grounds and wherever they have crawled and hopped while growing up, now take to the air together and, borne by the breeze, migrate for hundreds of miles. Like planes they take off into the wind but, once gaining altitude, fly with it, darkening the sky as far as one can see, and filling the air with the mighty hum of their countless miniature propellers.

You might think the region they left behind would

be free of grasshoppers and that farmers would not be bothered by them for a good long time. But they don't all leave. While still small, many wander away by themselves, seeming to prefer solitude to the crowds on the hatching grounds. Living in comparative peace and quiet, they grow up looking and acting quite unlike the ones that stay together. So different are they, not only in disposition but in size, shape, and color, that for a long time they were not suspected of being children of the same parents.

There seems to be something about the constant turmoil among the crowded grasshoppers that causes them to grow bigger and possibly tougher, and with longer, stronger wings than their stay-at-home brothers and sisters.

Some people claim that when an extra hard winter is on the way, the fur of animals grows heavier to match the coming weather. When summer ponds are drying up, the extra warmth hurries the turning of tadpoles into frogs. Where a condition develops in nature which promises no good for certain creatures, another condition may develop in the creatures themselves that saves them from destruction.

With the over-crowded grasshoppers it seems probable that many or all might starve unless millions migrated elsewhere. This might not happen the first dry summer. But after three or four dry summers in a row, with every female laying and almost all eggs hatching, and with plants growing ever more poorly, the food supply on the home grounds surely would be exhausted.

This looks like cause enough for the great swarms to travel. Nature does seem to have a plan that automatically gives the majority of these grasshoppers better flying equipment, when crowding makes it desirable that they move to other feeding grounds. But sometimes it seems as though a plan in nature, which may have been just the thing to save some kind of creature from dying out completely, keeps right on working after conditions have changed and the plan isn't needed any more.

So it may be with the migratory grasshoppers of the arid West. Perhaps very long ago their flights eastward saved their kind from dying out through starvation. They are to be found in many lush regions of the country now, regions which rarely if ever are so stricken by drought that traveling swarms develop. East of the great plains all these grasshoppers grow up to be the stay-at-home kind with the smaller wings, the different shape and color. However, in the West swarms still gather and go on long journeys, even to some extent in summers when there is still plenty to eat at home.

Scientists have found these travelers to be very fat, so fat that there is hardly room left inside their armor for their stomachs and other digestive organs. So evidently they are not traveling to find better feeding grounds. And as for seeking new lands for the laying of their eggs, they often settle in most unsuitable places. They may fly for as much as three days and nights without stopping unless forced to land by a sudden change of weather, especially rain. But otherwise, far from seeing on the earth below a favorable spot and electing to make it their new home, they apparently stop flying only because their fuel supply has given out, their fat is all used up, and they are hungry again.

This is a good enough reason for coming down to earth, but a very hit-or-miss one as far as self-preservation goes. They may land in a worse piece of country than the one they left, or on the roofs and pavements of a city, or in some big body of water where they drown.

Scientists are not finally agreed on just why these grasshoppers continue this often useless performance.

But from the eggs of stay-at-homes in the West, millions still hatch which grow up with the proper wings and disposition to travel far from home.

To farmers, wherever they come down, the hungry grasshoppers are invading enemies, air-borne troops, each insect a plane and a saboteur of terrible ability, fully equipped to cause destruction while living off the country. For they fill the fields, eating every inch of grass, grain, and vegetables down to the very roots, and stripping the leaves and even some of the bark from trees and bushes. I didn't know, as a boy, that sometimes grasshoppers really do chew tobacco. But if the migrating millions happen to light in a tobacco field, they go to work immediately, as ready really to chew and swallow tobacco as they are a lot of other things. They chew clothes on the line to shreds and even enter houses to make a ravenous meal of curtains, table linen, bedding, cotton or wool, dye colors and all.

Once, back in the eighteen-seventies, such destructive swarms of grasshoppers traveled eastward for so many summers in succession, on the westerly winds from the Rocky Mountain regions, that thousands of farms on the plains and prairies had to be abandoned. It was about as bad as the dust-bowl days of recent times, when grasshopper troubles were added to ruinous drought, as they often are. Grasshoppers swarmed along the railroad lines, causing engine wheels to spin on the tracks. Trains were delayed for hours or, if al-

ready under way, could not stop though engineers opened the sand-valves wide. Much of the sand glanced off the crowding grasshoppers' backs and never reached the rails. So trains went slithering past their stations while the platforms grew more slippery than if covered with banana peelings, under the feet of would-be passengers. In the summer of 1937, in eastern

44

Colorado, motor traffic came to a standstill when grasshoppers caused such skidding that travel was impossible. Such damage was done to crops that the Civilian Conservation Corps, the Works Progress Administration, and even the National Guard was called out to help the farmers conquer the insects.

West of the Rockies, California has had her grasshopper troubles, and similar things have happened in the eastern states though not on such a scale. Here many grasshoppers, flying too far with offshore winds, have found themselves out over the open sea. And ships' captains have found themselves carrying hordes of non-paying and most unwelcome passengers whose presence made the slanting decks most difficult to walk upon. Millions of the grasshoppers, having "missed their boat" and fallen into the water, if not eaten up by the gulls and fishes, were washed up dead in endless rows along the beaches.

There have been bad grasshopper plagues in India, southern Europe, and in Russia. And now and then the countries in Central and South America have grasshopper troubles too. In Argentina, for a recent example, freight trains had to be shortened and engines supplied with ten times the usual amount of sand or with rubber brushes to sweep the tracks. And in many parts of Africa seemingly endless throngs of flying grasshoppers appear from time to time. They land in such masses that their weight breaks the branches of big trees. There must be an awful mess when millions of African army ants happen to be where they come down. That would be another ant and grasshopper story Aesop wouldn't know about.

Conditions being just right, with the weather favoring and too few enemies to check them, grasshoppers, like other creatures, can become too numerous and a nuisance, to put it mildly. Weather favorable to grasshoppers is just the kind that doesn't favor farmers. When spring rains are scanty, no young grasshoppers drown underground at hatching time. They all come up, sometimes thousands from one square foot of soil. But a dry spring is bad for crops. They come up poorly if at all. Thus more grasshoppers nearly always appear when there is less to feed upon. For this reason they begin migrating before they can fly. There have been times when miles of prairie fires, set to stop them, have been smothered and put out by the forward ranks of half-grown grasshoppers, the far more numerous survivors crawling onward over the charred bodies of their dead comrades. These youngsters hop and crawl from field to field as they grow till after their last molt, when the air becomes their highway for as high as twelve thousand feet and as far as a thousand miles or more sometimes.

There were a few too many grasshoppers along part of the Mason-Dixon line in 1918, as I remember. When the troops, with which I was moving north from Dixie, spread out in the pastures of a beautiful farm in Virginia for the mid-day meal, grasshoppers crawled and jumped into our soup and coffee so fast we could scarcely drink it. A dozen would dunk themselves in the hot liquid and start to die while you were brushing another dozen off your bread to bite it. It was scoop them out and swallow fast or go without. I saw several soldiers tip their coffee onto the ground, disgusted, but a really hungry man can eat and drink even under worse conditions if he has to.

In fact those grasshoppers would have been welcomed as a choice addition to our bill of fare had we been a band of old-time American Indians. Out on those same prairies where I used to run and scare the grasshoppers, Potawatomis and Kickapoos would gather them for food. Some of the people would dig a big hole, perhaps four feet deep and eight feet wide, or thereabouts. Then everyone in the Indian encampment, from tiny tots to old granddads and grannies, formed a circle a half-mile from one side to the other, with the big hole in its center. Slowly all walked toward the hole beating the grass with sticks and frightening the grasshoppers ahead of them with shouts and

gestures. By the time everybody had gathered about the hole it was filled with their future food.

For the women would mix ground-up grasshoppers with acorn meal and make most nourishing patties, roasted on hot stones. And many grasshoppers were dried in the sun for winter use. Not long ago I broiled a big fat grasshopper just to see how it would taste. It turned red like lobster and the "drumsticks" tasted like it, too. They were the only parts I really liked, but I would have enjoyed a heaping plate of those.

48

However, it is simpler to stick to turkey. Let the turkey gobble grasshoppers all summer and fall, and you'll have the most delicious drumsticks to enjoy, come Thanksgiving Day.

Many Indian tribes harvested grasshoppers for food whenever they were plentiful, as other kinds of people in the Old World have in the past, and as some do still. For the insects we call grasshoppers in America are the short-feelered kind, which makes them locusts, like the ones that came as a plague to Egypt back in Bible times.

But even then, as today, the people made the best of locust plagues by using the insects to keep body and soul together. One of the wisest men who ever lived, Moses, named three kinds of locusts and a cricket which his hungry people could safely eat while wandering in the wilderness, a wilderness almost totally devoid of bigger game. John the Baptist, likewise wandering in the wilderness, ate locusts with wild honey, as doubtless many another man has done.

Arabs catch great quantities of locust grasshoppers and feed them, raw or roasted, to their camels, not disdaining a dish of this insect meat themselves. In Central Africa the Negroes run out in the cool of early morning, before the swarming locusts are warmed up enough to fly, and gather them in gourds and baskets for a feast.

The Japanese, planning a war to conquer the world but knowing they might have to stand a siege some day, studied all the kinds of food possible to obtain right there on their little island. This included every flower and weed and various insects. The Japanese diet doctors learned that grasshoppers are even more nourishing than fish, which is very good food indeed.

Japanese grasshoppers are cooked in soya bean oil and the diner picks them from his plate and pops them into his mouth.

Of course it's too much to expect most of us to take to such a diet while there is still anything else to eat. Our farmers could hardly hope to harvest a grasshopper crop and sell it as they would have sold the crops the grasshoppers ruined. So they fight them with every means available. In the hilly East poisoned mash is practical, sprinkled through the infested field. The dead insects have been at times so numerous as to form good fertilizer for the next year's crops.

Poison is used in the West as well, but there the land lies level and hopper-dozers can be employed. These are long troughs, on wheels or runners, in which water covered by a thin layer of oil is driven through the standing crops. At the back of the trough is a high frame covered with canvas. The frightened grasshoppers leap either into the rolling trough or hit the canvas behind it and then fall in. A little oil in their breathing portholes soon smothers them.

A Hopper-dozer

Grasshoppers destroyed thus may be used to fertilize the fields, the amount of oil being very slight. But some farmers make another device somewhat like a hopper-dozer but which captures the swarming enemy without using chemicals. A hopper-catcher in Utah collected forty bushels in a few hours which were used the following winter as feed for hens, greatly increasing their output of eggs.

Perhaps you can get a good idea of what a battle it is some years to save our food from grasshoppers if I say that in one summer they destroyed nearly ninety million dollars' worth of it in spite of about 27,000 tons of poison used to stop them. The government sent 462 carloads of poison to Nebraska alone and even that was not enough. It costs a lot, but would cost far more if we did nothing about it. For every dollar spent to fight the grasshoppers we save about fifty-seven dollars' worth of food. And of course, though grasshoppers may be the worst crop destroyers, there are other insect pests to battle too. Various kinds of worms, weevils, moths, and beetles by the billion, cost us a pretty penny to control year after year.

Grasshoppers have their share of diseases and parasites, such as red lice and hair-worms which live on and in them and finally cause their deaths. But such things have to become epidemics to cut down the number of grasshoppers enough to make much difference, and this only develops once in a very long while.

A good way to prevent the number of grasshoppers from becoming too numerous in the first place is to plow the land after they have laid their eggs in the fall, thus burying millions of them before they are born. Sometimes planes fly over infested fields spraying poison dust on the young grasshoppers and the crops they are feeding on. The poison washes away with the first rain but by then the insects are largely done for.

Our great farming regions are like a vast table set for grasshoppers to enjoy. At the same time, because the land is settled, many of the grasshoppers' natural enemies (which could help us to prevent their prosper-

ing so at our expense) have been killed or scared away to wilder places. Almost any kind of bird that's big enough to manage them will eat grasshoppers in midsummer, no matter what its usual feeding habits are. I have seen great blue herons leave their fishing to join crows in the fields, filling their crops with grasshoppers.

But these big bashful birds are not as common in farming country as they were when that same land was wild. Most kinds of wild poultry are either scarce or entirely absent for hundreds of miles where they once were found in numbers. So are the small grasshopper-eating hawks and many other kinds of birds. Frogs, toads and salamanders, snakes and lizards, all great

grasshopper eaters, tend to disappear from settled places. So do skunks, foxes, shrews, ground-squirrels, and the various kinds of field and wood mice. It is our own doing, so now we have to fight against grasshoppers and a host of other insect pests without the aid of these allies. And even as we fight the grasshoppers, if we use poisoned bait we probably kill many helpful creatures which try it too, or which eat the poisoned insects while they are still alive.

Like almost any good thing, too much of it isn't anything good. But as a rule grasshoppers become too numerous only about once in twenty years or so. And all in between those times they are, as we have seen, a very important item on the menu of many a creature. Even the house cat that is lucky enough to live in the country catches and eats grasshoppers. Many a kitten learns to hunt by stalking grasshoppers and crickets. And besides keeping the summer shopping basket full for other animals, grasshoppers add a certain lively pleasure to anybody who loves the open country, from the small boy racing over the fields to the aged man who leans upon a cane.

5

SOME KINDS OF GRASSHOPPERS IN PARTICULAR

LET me describe briefly a few of the grasshoppers you are most likely to meet within the boundaries of our country. Common from coast to coast and from Key West to Canada is the Carolina locust, a big grasshopper of the crackling kind. In fact it is the biggest kind of grasshopper in the northern states, females being over two inches long from forehead to the tips of their folded wings. The males, as with other locusts, are somewhat smaller. Probably it is called Carolina locust because the first man ever to write about it saw it there, as in the case of the Virginia deer and the Virginia horned owl, both of which are found in many other states than just Virginia.

The Carolina locust is also called the Quaker, because of the modest colors it wears, which vary from dusty brown to a dull slate gray, sometimes almost black. These are the colors that show when the grasshopper is at rest. They are a good deception for the eyes of its enemies, for this is one of those locusts that love the dusty road and the bare spots in poor pastures more than the green of grassy places, though you may

The
Carolina
Crepitator

find them there also. But they prefer to rest upon the ground where the same drab colors as their own prevail.

Not that the Carolina locust relies entirely on a good disguise for safety. Though dull of color, it is alert of brain and quick to fly at your approach. It is very much of a surprise package. Not only does this seeming bit of the very earth suddenly spring into the air and fly, loudly crackling, but it displays much unsuspected beauty. Its large spread wings are black with a wide pale yellow border, and very handsome. It is like a lady, outwardly plainly dressed, whose petticoats are astonishingly bright and fancy. This grasshopper and its closest kin are called the band-winged locusts.

Their hind legs are rather short as grasshopper hind legs go. But they are used more for launching their owners into the air than for hopping's sake alone. For these and some of their nearest relatives are the super-flyers of the grasshopper world. They go fast and far, zigzagging perhaps or in a great circle, landing almost on the spot from which they started, or suddenly cutting back from a long straight flight just before dropping to the ground. This latter seems intended to make their enemies uncertain of their exact location after landing. For once down on a patch of earth, they look like only one more lump of the same, or a very dead bit of wood. It is a "Now you see me—now you don't" performance.

There is another performance which the males put on repeatedly in late summer, apparently to impress the females. It is a "Look at me—am I not marvelous?" exhibition. First one male and then another leaps four or five feet into the air but goes no farther.

There he flies in place like a helicopter, a splendid stunt if you can do it. Some are more wobbly at it than others. Does the female really distinguish between the abilities of two rivals thus dancing in the air, trying to impress her? And does she also admire the coloring of their wings thus vividly displayed? It may be so.

The Carolina locust has handsome colors on its wings, but some of its close grasshopper cousins are still more striking as they fly. A number of these reverse the Carolina's color scheme, having yellow wings with a dark border or a band across them, adding also red on the hinder shins with black-tipped barbs. One wears wings of coral with a dark band to set them off like the leads in stained glass windows.

Three of these band-winged locusts are grasshoppers I should love to tell one thing about to that old fabulator, Aesop. The green-striped, the coral-winged, and the spring yellow-winged locusts may be exceptions to the rule, but they don't die when winter comes. Hatched in midsummer instead of in the spring, they have not reached their final molt by fall. Under the rubble beneath the meadow grass they creep, and there they sleep till winter's end. About May Day they molt again and get their wings, and mate and lay their eggs which, unlike other northern grasshopper eggs, need no freezing spell before they will hatch.

But most of all, Aesop ought to have been told about the little pygmy locusts, less than half an inch in length, which live through the winter in the grown-up state. He would have been amazed, not to say enlightened, in a January thaw to see hundreds of these little grasshoppers crawling from their beds beneath loose bark or from under haystacks, to sun themselves. Of course, some of them might die before spring if the end of a thaw should come too suddenly and catch them, not napping, but out for a walk. But enough would survive to show old Aesop that his fable was founded on ignorance of a few of the facts.

In country rambles one sometimes meets some of the slant-faced locusts face to face. They are lively leapers and fairly good flyers of medium size. They perch so exclusively on plants that they are often found in flooded places, perfectly contented as long as the water doesn't rise too high. The fact that it covers the ground below is no concern of theirs. Of course, unlike ground-loving Carolina locusts, they have large sticky footpads for nonskid landings on smooth leaves and grass blades after every hop and flight.

But the most peculiar thing about them is the form of their faces, which slant rapidly backward like the

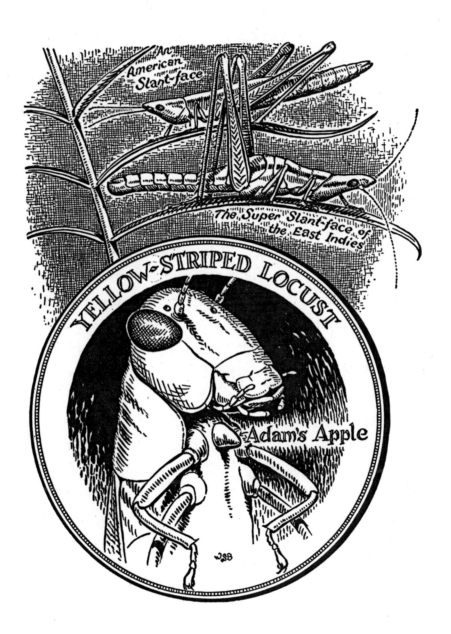

An American Slant-face

The Super Slant-face of the East Indies

YELLOW-STRIPED LOCUST

Adam's Apple

noses of some of our fighting planes. If this gives them some special advantage, no one knows what it may be. They don't·seem to get through the air any faster than the more blunt-faced boys. People with receding chins and foreheads sometimes talk faster than those with big brows and bulldog jaws. But they may merely speak more nonsense in the same amount of time. Streamlined faces are not necessarily an advantage to them. Probably the same is true of slant-faced locusts; they just happen to have fast-looking faces.

Naturally some of the commonest grasshoppers are the most troublesome from a human point of view; the more common, the more troublesome. Some of these are the migratory kinds whose damaging doings have been described; and some are simply speedy multipliers that stay in one locality.

Because it tells in the Bible that Adam was the first man and that he committed the first sin, we sometimes say of a troublesome person that it is the "old Adam" in him which makes him act that way. So it is funny to find that all these especially troublesome grasshoppers, though not descendants of Adam, do have Adam's apples, a feature missing among less pestiferous kinds. On the throat of each, male and female, there is a small cone-like projection, the purpose of which has never been discovered. Perhaps it actually serves no purpose, just as there seems to be no special need for real Adam's apples, men with big ones or men with nearly none being able to swallow with equal ease. At any rate, this little lump on the throats of these grasshoppers serves to set them apart from other kinds.

None of these grasshoppers can fiddle, having neither rasps nor ridges on legs or wings. Nevertheless they have ears to hear, and both males and females make all the motions of fiddling sometimes. Perhaps they charm each other with the color flashing from their fiddlesticks, often brilliant red, as much as they otherwise might with music.

These grasshoppers rustle as they fly but cannot crepitate—a fancy word for fancy crackling. Like the slant-faced locusts, they have much larger sticking pads on their feet than the Carolina locusts, being lovers of lush green vegetation. One of this group is that wingless thicket-haunting grasshopper, common in cool regions. It is a dark, dingy green, with markings of black and white.

The other kinds, all with propeller wings more or less transparent, are colored mostly to resemble grass either green or faded yellow-brown, or both. A general olive coloring is relieved here and there by brighter hues (on the underside especially, which may be a yellow-green or yellow), and by patterns of dusky brown or black. The brightest colors are on the big hind shins and on the inner side of the thighs. These may be yellow or blue but are still more often red and, like the undersides, hardly noticeable when the legs are folded as the insects rest.

Perhaps the prettiest of the lot is the red-legged locust whose name does not distinguish it very much from various other Adam's-apple-owning grasshoppers. What does set it off is the daring color worn on its head and back, a rich rose, most of the time in sharp contrast to the green of its habitat. This locust and the two far-traveling kinds—the lesser migratory and the Rocky Mountain migratory locusts—look a lot alike, the latter being the largest of the three.

But there is still a larger kind which goes on the rampage once in a while. The yellow-striped or two-striped locust is slimmer than the big Carolinas, but its body is almost as long and it has much longer jumping legs. It has been very troublesome at times in Minnesota and Vermont, and may be found from New England to the Pacific, and as far south as North Carolina. The color of its mighty shins varies from region to region and between individuals. Shins in the middle states may be brown, yellow, blue-green, or red.

In New England only the red-shins have been seen. But I had one of these grasshoppers here in the Cats-kills with bright yellow shins which after a few weeks turned to red. As grasshoppers grow older, their colors tend to deepen. Those that live through several frosts turn very dark and have an oily look all over, like farm machinery smeared with grease before being put away for winter.

Winter puts most of them away all right, but in the South certain kinds of grasshoppers may be seen throughout the year. There are the Adam's-apple-bearing American and differential locusts, both of which have been bad southern crop destroyers at times. And then there are two notable non-Adam's-apple-bearing grasshoppers, the lubber locusts of the Southeast and Southwest, great heavy-bodied insects with very stubby wings. Though there are locusts in the deep tropics with wider wingspread and longer bodies, probably none are quite as heavy and bulky as these lubbers of our warmer states.

In other lands live other kinds of locusts with similar characteristics that vary with various climates. In Argentina, where weather is rather like our own, they likewise have grasshopper wars to wage on their mighty plains and pampas.

There is one kind of grasshopper in that country which not only hops and flies for safety but which imitates, in its coloring, the steel blue and chocolate body and the red wings of a certain poisonous and foul-

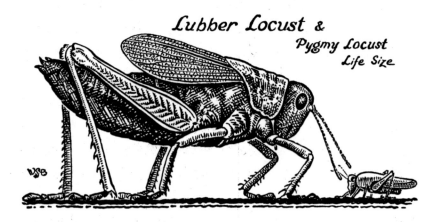

Lubber Locust &
Pygmy Locust
Life Size

smelling wasp. And though it doesn't imitate the odor, it acts so like the wasp that altogether its enemies frequently are fooled into leaving it alone. If you pick one up it swings the end of its abdomen around as though to sting. You are very likely to let go before you realize that this grasshopper has nothing with which to hurt you on that end, though at the other end it is a most copious spitter of "tobacco juice." Probably birds and other grasshopper hunters have the same reaction.

66

Some large Brazilian locusts are so completely camouflaged in the shape and color of their wings that they even have patches to imitate decay and mildew. Thus they escape the creatures that devour insects and likewise look unappetizing to those that feed on leaves. Others rely on an exactly opposite device for their protection, their colors being gaudy and conspicuous. These seem to indicate that they may taste terrible or are poisonous, therefore needing no disguise—a warning that is false.

Amidst the gray-greens and dull browns of thornbrush and cactus in the Galapagos Islands, I have seen great grasshoppers which looked as though just painted with the brightest of enamels. Perhaps this causes the Galapagos hawks to hesitate, though they snatch up great black centipedes at least eight inches long without a qualm.

In the never ending struggle to preserve their lives, grasshoppers turn the tables on one class of enemy to some extent. Most kinds of mice, in America at least, will eat grasshoppers now and then, and one kind, called the grasshopper mouse, eats almost nothing else all summer. But in Africa there live large mouse grasshoppers. Not content with a vegetarian diet, they actually catch small mice and feast upon them.

As a matter of fact, grasshoppers in general, and crickets too, are pleased to vary their menu of greens with a bit of meat as opportunity affords. This is usually the dead body of another insect come upon by

African
Mouse-catcher

chance. But a grasshopper may consume a portion of itself. Strong though the hind legs are they break off easily. Indeed, it often seems that a grasshopper or a cricket purposely breaks off the leg you hold it by, as a fair price for freedom. But if you put it into a cage with plenty of food plus the severed leg, it is just as likely to dine on its own drumstick as on clover.

A cave-katydid, which went through its final molt in

68

my study, ate up all its cast-off armor excepting the very spiny lower half of its big hind shins. This was about the same sort of self-cannibalism as biting one's fingernails, except that the cuticle covered its entire body.

6

KATYDIDS AND CRICKETS

IT IS the katydid and cricket that really do the finest fiddling, though perhaps old Aesop's fable has made the grasshopper more famous for it. Most of the insect music that we hear in summertime is made by these two more talented relations.

Now the names of grasshoppers and katydids and crickets are confused and most misleading. Names given them by ordinary mortals like you and me are all mixed up with the names applied by scientists. And the scientific names seem badly muddled up amongst themselves. We are told that the insects we call grasshoppers are more truly locusts. True grasshoppers, the scientists assert, are katykids, and cave-crickets are really katydids which live in caves. Yet katydids, which are not locusts, have the scientific name Locustidae, meaning "of the locust family." Incidentally the so-called seventeen-year locusts aren't locusts but cicadas, sap-sucking bugs.

All this is much too complicated, except perhaps for scientists. And so I'm going to risk making confusion worse confounded by trying now to simplify it all, that is for the convenience of our simpler-minded selves. The insects most of us call grasshoppers have, among other features, much shorter feelers than insects almost anyone would label katydids. Some of the latter are known as meadow grasshoppers, but to anyone who has ever seen a tree-katydid or a bush-katydid, these slender-legged, long-feelered insects from the fields are meadow-katydids. And the so-called cave-crickets are wingless katydids which live in caves. So cave-katydids let us call them, reserving the name of cricket for insects that really are crickets.

After the spring peepers and trilling toads have ended their great choruses, and after the birds have been singing for some time, more and more the insect instrumentalists take up the tune. By mid-summer, when many birds have ceased their singing, the grasshoppers and katydids and crickets are in a great crescendo that goes on day and night with never an interruption. Theirs is the greatest orchestra on earth. It's stupendous, it's colossal! It reaches from the tropics to the Arctic and from sea to sea. It plays from dawn to dark to dawn, and on and on. A few dozen players may stop fiddling as you pass along, but billions more continue undisturbed. As some take time out for their meals and rest, others fall to work with renewed energy. There are no union hours and no dues. All insects

which have instruments may play as much or little as they please, however good or bad musicians they may be.

Actually, of course, the insects are not interested in orchestral playing, each one only intent on making itself heard. Nevertheless insect music is like that of a mighty orchestra in that it is produced with instruments by many players, all following a great conductor. This conductor is a temperamental fellow, familiar to

72

us all. His name is Old Man Weather. With many variations on the theme he may call for pianissimo with a sudden chill in one section, while working up fortissimo with furious heat in another. At the end of the piece he compels diminuendo and finally silence, with a wave of his frosty fingers in the fall.

Clearly and often loudly though the insects play, people who live in the country are apt not to hear them even after dark, when daytime noises have quieted down, unless they listen purposely. For, like dinner music which sets everybody talking, this insect playing rarely interrupts our rural thoughts while possibly it stimulates them. The "chirping of the bugs" is so over-stimulating to some city people, who never before have heard these noisy relatives of the silent cockroach, that they have to go back to the clamor they are used to for a good night's sleep.

As with grasshoppers, it is only male katydids and crickets that play, and, by his fiddling, each expresses his emotions whatever they may be. Sometimes, as when a human being whistles, it is perhaps just happiness and his own good health. Sometimes he may be trying to enchant a female; but if he responds to the playing of another male it is only to outdo him if he can, and probably never to join in a duet.

Each kind of insect has its own peculiar noise that it makes repeatedly with very little variation. It is not easy to describe most of these sounds so that the reader will recognize them readily, but here are a few:

The large oblong-winged tree katydid seems to say, "Zzzzzz-Ipswich!" over and over.

The fork-tailed bush katydid goes, "Zeep—zeep—zeep," slowly now and then.

The sword-bearing conehead katydid of the fields "zips" rapidly with never a pause, like a minute sewing machine on an endless seam.

The robust conehead katydid sounds like a small cicada with a fairly loud and steady "bizz" drawn out for many minutes.

The common meadow katydid does several soft "zeees" in a row, ever more rapidly, then hits high "zeeee" and holds it.

Such notes, plus the miniature police whistles of field crickets, the soft purrs and long toad-like trills or the endless "Re-treat, re-treat" of various tree crickets, the peeper-like "chirrups" of bush crickets, and the deeper froggy "churps" of mole-crickets, with a day-time grasshopper obligato, these, with the sounds of many others, make up the music of the Insect Symphony Society's annual concert.

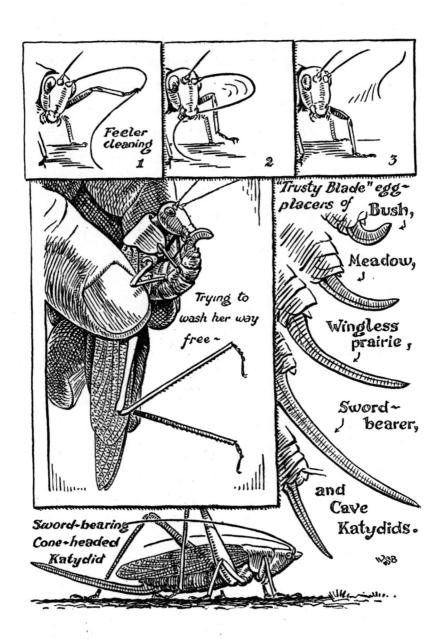

Feeler
cleaning
1

2

3

"Trusty Blade" egg-
placers of Bush,

Meadow,

Trying to
wash her way
free ~

Wingless
prairie,

Sword-
bearer,

and
Cave
Katydids.

Sword-bearing
Cone-headed
Katydid

W.B

But louder than all others in the nighttime playing is the broad-winged or leaf-winged katydid. All the rest play but a poor second fiddle to this one, which carries on the whole night long with the noise that sounds like "Katy did!" and "Katy did! She did!"

Now Katy's deed undoubtedly was done a very long time ago, for these insects have been telling about it for as long as English-speaking people can remember, in fact much longer. They were saying "Katy did" before either of these two words belonged to human language.

Whatever it was that the unidentified but over-active Katy so definitely did do, we are never told. Of course, it may have been something too terrible to mention.

There are people who claim that some of the insects say "Katy didn't, she didn't, didn't!" But it's not worth arguing about as long as no one knows what she is supposed to have or not to have done. Listen to their racket in the trees on late summer evenings and decide for yourself who says what and who is ahead and, if possible, who is right. Probably both sides are, the did-ders and the didn'ters. Katy doubtless did a lot of things, and there were things she didn't do.

In New England many people say that Katy isn't

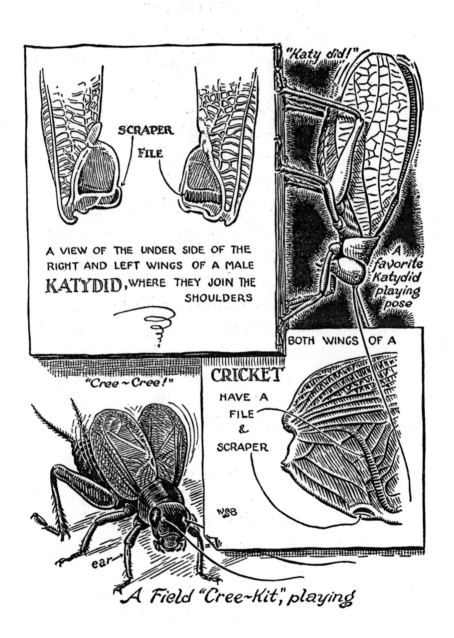

"Katy did!"

SCRAPER

FILE

A VIEW OF THE UNDER SIDE OF THE RIGHT AND LEFT WINGS OF A MALE KATYDID, WHERE THEY JOIN THE SHOULDERS

A favorite Katydid playing pose

"Cree~Cree!"

CRICKET
HAVE A
FILE
&
SCRAPER

BOTH WINGS OF A

ear

A Field "Cree~Kit," playing

even mentioned, that the katydids simply squawk three times, and let it go at that. And in the South the calls of katydids are not considered English either. Their name down there is Cackle-Jack.

As far as I am concerned, their rasping sounds are like the creaking of old-fashioned buggy springs, or even like some of the body squeaks in modern cars. Perhaps this is only natural since all these sounds are produced by one unlubricated surface rubbing on another. Unlike grasshoppers, katydids and crickets do not use their legs in fiddling, but play on one wing with the other. In the katydid's case it's the left wing with its file-like row of ridges rubbing over the right wing with its hard little scraper just behind the shoulders, where the wings overlap. From there the wings bulge backward on either side and act as amplifiers. Usually the tattle-tale music is made with the performer facing head down along a leaf or twig, the wings slightly ajar, just free of the body.

The cricket plays in almost any position but with its right wing over its left, though there appears to be an equally good file and scraper on either wing. Maybe it can reverse and play like a katydid when its wings grow weary in the customary cricket posture. Maybe there is about the same proportion of "left-handed" crickets as there are left-handed people.

Katydids and crickets have a slit in each front shin. Inside are air spaces and eardrums, and these are the hearing apparatus with which one katydid or cricket listens to another. Some female insects seem to have ears only for the "voice" of the male. But katydids must have their receiving sets tuned to other things as well, for they stop their own noise at the sound of your voice or even your footfall underneath their tree.

Though cautious in this way, katydids are calmer and not as jumpy as grasshoppers. We seldom disturb or even see the broad-winged katydids, because of their preference for the tops of trees. It seems to be their attitude that katydids should not be seen, but heard. Many are not even seen by the ever-hungry, sharp-eyed birds, because they are so leaf-like both in shape and color. Often all they have to do to escape detection is sit still.

If a bird does see a katydid and makes ready for a meal, the big green insect suddenly swells and rasps right in its enemy's face. This may be enough to scare away the smaller birds. And if, on a rare occasion, you may meet this high-tree katydid close at hand and pick it up, it will surely try to bite you.

The usual movements of a katydid are minus any

79

sign of haste. Climbing among the leaves, it picks up each foot separately and sets it down deliberately. Even when it jumps it takes plenty of time getting set and aimed exactly so. Though katydids jump very well, they don't develop the power of the more compact grasshoppers. Probably the legs are too long, the feet too far from the knees to get the strongest leverage. It is this longness which makes for much of the slow motion of katydids. Try tapping the ground as fast as you can with two sticks, one much longer than the other, and you will see.

On the other hand, because of the cricket's sizable but more muscular-looking legs, we might expect it to jump as well as the grasshopper and better than the katydid. But though quick, it is so loose in its joints and in the very use it makes of its legs, that it is the poorest jumper of the three. Its jumps are very shallow so that it rarely rises more than a few inches above the ground and therefore travels no more than a foot or two at best.

But crickets are the speediest swimmers of the three, probably because they are runners more than the other two. An effort to run in the water results in more successful swimming than trying to jump through it as the grasshopper does, or slowly walking through it, as does

one kind of katydid at least. I watched a meadow katydid that had fallen into a pond walk-swim to a stick
projecting from the surface. Here it was still six inches
from the shore. But instead of jumping the distance, it
deliberately launched itself again and made it by
water. At least it had the life-preserving virtue of
keeping calm on falling overboard.

Crickets, always nervous and lively, run almost
more than they jump, but sometimes even the dilatory
katydid will run at least a little way along a branch,
in a most exaggerated manner. Tilting low in front
and high behind, wings slightly raised, it hurries forward like an angry brood-hen defending her flock. But
almost immediately it stops. Unlike the grasshopper
which puts the whole foot down, the katydid holds up
its end claws like the little fingers of our more fas-
tidious diners.

Katydids seem almost over-nice about the state of
their feet, cleaning them in the mouth very frequently.
But being leaf dwellers, their three sticky pads on each
foot are especially well developed, and probably pick
up dust particles continually. Their sense of touch is
doubtless very delicate so that, like the Princess and
the Pea, they feel every little thing.

The very long feelers of katydids and crickets cannot be cleaned, like those of the "short-horned" grass-hoppers, between one foot and the ground. Instead these insects reach out with one foot and pull the feeler on that side close to the face, putting it into the mouth. Jaws and tongue then give it a good going-over as it slowly is drawn through to its tip and snaps up clean.

Tree katydids you are more likely to see than the broad-winged kind are the oblong-winged and angular-winged katydids, large and very trusting insects that like our human neighborhoods and often perch in the vines or on the screens of houses. They expect no harm at our hands, and one can be picked up by the folded wings as easily as if it were in fact one of the green leaves it resembles. Even then such a katydid does not suspect that it is you who has deprived it of its freedom.

Recently I held a female angular-winged katydid by the wings, restraining also her long hind legs lest she break one off as crickets and grasshoppers will do to free themselves. She did not appear to connect me with her predicament, realizing only that she was snagged somehow. She evidently felt that a general clean-up might clear away the entanglement. She didn't spit in fear or anger but used her clear saliva to wash in mid-air her forefeet and shins as far as she could reach and the upper part of these legs starting at the shoulder. Her elbows were out of reach of her mouth. She bent her face way down and licked her

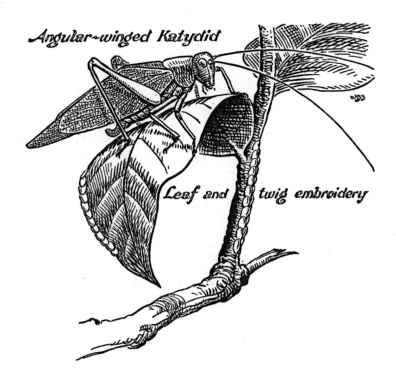

Angular-winged Katydid

Leaf and twig embroidery

chest, then bent her abdomen up, gripping it with two forefeet and one middle foot and washed her egg-placer. Then I set her down, and doubtless she was satisfied that she had gotten herself out of a mysterious mess by her own efforts. She was in no hurry to get away and only jumped and flew after I had poked her

83

hinder shins a half dozen times.

The eggs of katydids are laid in the fall and hatch in the spring. Their egg-placers are remarkable to see. Though hollow, all suggest some sort of weapon, resembling, in the different kinds, pruning knives, sickles, scimitars, swords, and daggers. The first three of these designs are flat and curved affairs of varying lengths, carried by such as the green angular-winged, oblong-winged, bush, and meadow katydids. The swords, as long as their owners' bodies, are worn by the sword-bearing cone-headed katydids, also meadow dwellers. And the daggers, belonging to the brown and the albino cave-katydids, are actually diggers for planting eggs in the earth.

Tree, bush, and meadow katydids place their precious packages in portions of the plants they live upon. Some, like the cone-heads, lay between the stems and sheaths of meadow grasses. Some, like the broad-wings, use crevices in the soft bark of trees. Others, such as the angular-wings, embroider the edges of leaves or twigs with rows of cucumber-seed-shaped eggs neatly overlapping. These are held in place by just the right amount of glue, which substance is exuded in the egg-laying of all katydids and crickets, though in no such quantity as with grasshoppers.

The eggs of the fork-tailed bush katydids are very flat at first. They have to be because they are placed between the upper and lower layers of a single leaf. Grasping the leaf with her forefeet, the bush-katydid bites away some of the rim. Then, holding her egg-placer in her jaws to guide it, she does a job more difficult than threading a fine needle, after many misses finally getting the egg-placer between the two halves of the leaf. An egg is released and the placer withdrawn. Sometimes she puts as many as five eggs in a row before selecting a new location. The flat eggs soon swell, producing little bulges as the leaf heals over them.

The cave-katydids, pale with brown markings, which live in one of my insect cages, started laying eggs in August and were still at it in the middle of October. When about to lay, a female scrabbles at the dirt in front of her, pushing it back beneath her with forefeet, farther back with her middle feet, and kicking it out behind with her big hind legs. She does not appear to be trying to dig a hole. After a few nervous minutes of this, she reaches out with all six legs, grasping bits of rubble as though to guy herself down like a tent in a storm, and brings her dagger egg-placer (which usually points backward like a tail) up under her till it points straight down.

Twisting and turning her body, she drills into the loam till all of the egg-placer is out of sight. She raises it and lowers it six or seven times, still twisting, feeling for the best spot between dirt particles below for

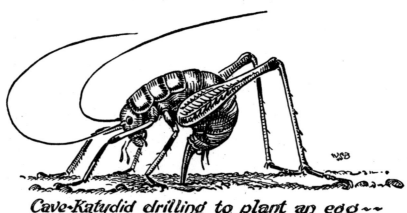

Cave-Katydid drilling to plant an egg ~~

the single egg. Satisfied at last, with egg-placer thrust clear down, she sits very still for half a minute. Presently the two little tails at the end of her body quiver slightly. Then up she gets, for the slender egg is now in the ground, well planted.

As her egg-placer moved in and out of the earth like the needle of a sewing machine, she was herself in fact a sowing machine, planting katydid seed. An inch away she does it all over again, though with far less frantic scrabbling at the start. She may deposit half a dozen eggs this way and several more upon the morrow. This performance takes place in August, September, and October, and for all I know it may happen again before a real hard freeze sets in. Thus, though these cave-katydids lay few eggs at a time, they do so several times a season. It is possible that, living somewhat sheltered lives, such grasshopper relatives do not die after one season, but survive the winter and lay more eggs the next year.

Their notion of a cave is any dark enclosure, preferably a trifle damp, and they leave their forest nooks to live in our cellar. They dash into a mouse hole when I open the tool closet door, a dangerous refuge if the mouse should feel like eating them. One even went up through the walls to the attic and, trying the bait in a circular mouse trap there, ended its career in strange surroundings.

These cave-katydids are most pugnacious. On their long hind legs are large and wicked-looking spurs, used by the males in some fancy dueling. This they carry on in rounds, often half an hour long, with rest periods for eating mushrooms or mildewed fruit and such choice morsels, and for seeking favor with the females.

Sometimes when one male, walking around an object, comes suddenly face to face with another, he will charge, fiercely striking out with his front feet as if to seize the other just behind the head. The other never faces this style of attack but leaps as though for his very life.

But if, as happens most of the time, each sees the other from a little distance so that there can be no element of surprise, they go at each other rear end to, fencing with their great hind legs. Apparently they see very well what they are doing with their compound eyes, and I notice they are careful to keep their thin long delicate feelers forward and out of harm's way.

They don't kick at each other as the females sometimes do, but jab savagely as though to tear the tender and thinly armored body of the rival with their big sharp barbs. On these same spikes each catches and parries the thrusts of the other, if not on the first and longest barbs, then farther up the shins on smaller ones, where also the power of the rival's stroke is partly spent already, as a rule.

But once in a while a jab is so swift and furious that the striking leg zips past the other fellow's guard and even rakes at his head for the fraction of a second, endangering the feelers, often more important to a cavekatydid than its eyes. "Never turn your back on an

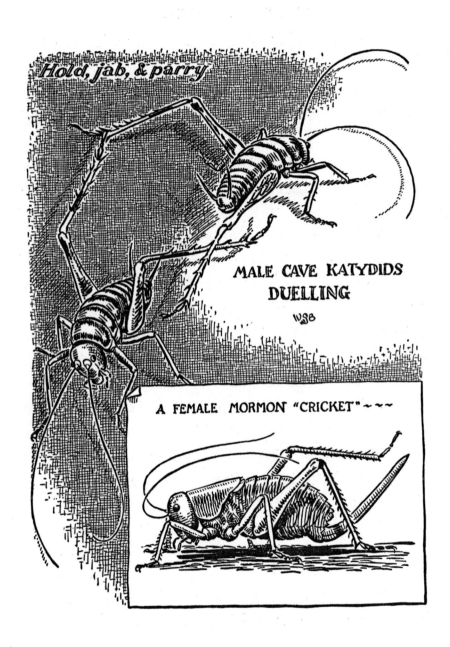

Hold, jab, & parry

MALE CAVE KATYDIDS
DUELLING

W.S.

A FEMALE MORMON "CRICKET" ~ ~ ~

opponent" is a rule observed in reverse in their style of boxing.

They do a lot of holding too, each gripping one of his rival's hind legs in his own rear claws while trying to shake his other leg free from the rival's grip, to land another blow. Often, while holding and watching for the slightest weakening of the other's grip, they back closer and closer together till their great legs are spread, it would seem, to the breaking point.

But though they have fought so fiercely, on the ground, up the walls, and upside down on the ceiling of the cage almost every day for three full months, not one has suffered any injury as far as I can see. It seems to be almost a sport with these energetic insects, serious though their rivalries may be. I am inclined to think that to really do each other in, a battle jaw to jaw would be the thing. And evidently none of them wishes to take this risk unless at an instant of surprise when, as I say, only the surpriser is willing, the surprised always leaping out of the way.

I think these cave-katydids live quite happily in their cage. By nature they prefer enclosures and never try to get through the wires as grasshoppers, needing the great open spaces, will do to their dying day. With plenty of crannies in which to hide, room to chase each other, and lots to eat they are as healthy now as they were way back in June.

Being wingless, they are mute. And there is not the least hint of an ear on their forward shins where other katydids and crickets have them. Yet this may not mean that they are deaf. For while good reception on the radio does not interest them, they are shocked and scared by static. So, whereas they may fail to notice certain kinds of sounds, they keenly *feel* some others, though with what I cannot say. Perhaps their very long feelers, often called antennae, are actually aerials of a sort.

When nights are cool or cold, they gather on the ceiling of their sleeping box where the day's heat lingers longest, and where crowding conserves their bodies' warmth to some extent. They don't do this out of comradely concern for one another's welfare; each is acting on its own behalf exclusively. This brings them all into the same, the warmest corner, where they settle down only after much pushing and unceremonious shoving. The males may do a bit of spurring and sparring till finally all succumb to slumber. So they remain until the rising temperature next morning thaws them into another day's activity.

Out on the open plains west of the Mississippi are

various brown ground-loving katydids, wingless or nearly so, and much like cave-katydids in most respects. But they are great multipliers and, as if grasshopper plagues were not enough to drive the farmers crazy, these related insects, usually called Coulée

A SUMATRAN CRICKET

DOES HE LIVE TO SUPPORT HIS SUPPORTS?

crickets and Mormon crickets, sometimes do tremendous damage to the crops. In 1936, in Utah, vegetable farmers borrowed 84,000 turkeys from poultry farmers during a "cricket" plague. The big birds gobbled up the invading insects, saving the crops and returning to their owners all fattened up for market. Does the old-time phrase about killing two birds with one stone apply here? It was 84,000 birds and billions of "crickets."

7

CRICKETS IN PARTICULAR

SOME of the crickets, properly so-called, look quite a lot like some kinds of katydids and are their nearest relatives. Tree crickets have a katydidly look with their long feelers, egg-placers, and very long legs. But whereas katydid wings overlap a little just behind the shoulders, they lie otherwise along the sides of the body, only touching at their upper edges over most of the back. Cricket wings may cover the sides somewhat, but they overlap and lie flatly one upon the other for their entire length. Among the many kinds there are crickets with big wings, smaller wings, and no wings at all.

Crickets lay their eggs in as great a variety of places as do katydids. Tree crickets use the bark or pithy stems of the plants which they inhabit. Their egg-placers have a saw edge at the end for cutting into the tough material. Field crickets punch holes in the earth with their awl-like egg-placers. And mole-crickets lay their eggs in rooms hollowed out in their burrows underground.

Though katydids make much of the nighttime racket, crickets, as our ears feel it, make the more melodious noises. Not that it matters to the insects how it all sounds to us. It used to be asserted that because only male grasshoppers, katydids, and crickets could produce sounds, the sounds were made for the sole purpose of enchanting females.

But when I see my favorite field cricket making his morning rounds, touching this and that with his feelers, tickling a sleepy grasshopper till it jumps, cleaning up a bit, nibbling a little food, playing happy-sounding music all the while, I don't believe his feelings are romantic.

When the female comes out of her cardboard sleeping box, he greets her with some extra fine fiddling. But he may work up to such a pitch as to be almost speechless, his wings working feverishly but making only a dry rustling sound with now and then a feeble squeak. Perhaps, however, there are some lovely sounds she hears but which my human hearing fails to gather, some notes especially for her.

He almost always turns his back to play. I find that he sounds twice as loud facing away as facing toward

94

me. His raised wings amplify the sound like the flare of a megaphone.

He delights to fiddle in the outer half of a safety match box, increasing his volume tremendously, as some of us enjoy shouting in an echoing underpass. He seems to feel that the little half-a-box belongs to him, for he will tolerate the presence of no other insect in it. There are several grasshoppers in his cage which have made the mistake of crawling into that box. They weren't crawling when they left it.

The male tree and bush crickets have something more than just music with which to charm the females. On the back of each, beneath his wings, is a basin-like depression containing a sweet liquid. The females dote on this, and though they may have eaten nectar-filled aphids half the night, a whole dish of cricket candy is still irresistible.

The playing of his honeyed notes may not always be intended to attract a female, but certainly it serves to tell her where he is in the darkness, and at the same time, because his wings are always raised high in playing, she can help herself to some of his sweets. But a fiddling bush cricket male has been observed to act rather bothered by the arrival of a female with her everlasting sweet tooth. He edged away as though it was to him a nuisance that he couldn't get his wings up to play once in a while without some female coming around. As with my field cricket, a bush or tree cricket may make music for its own sake sometimes, or just because he feels all right.

The temperature has a lot to do with how they feel and how and when they fiddle. The ghostly pale snowy tree cricket is called the temperature cricket too, because by counting the number of notes he makes per minute you can figure within a few degrees how warm or cool it is. At 63° he does 100 chirps per minute, working faster with more heat or slowing down with less.

This musician works on the night shift mostly. But when I light a fire in my study stove in the chill of a mountain morning, and sit at the desk with my outdoor clothes still on, I can tell when the thermometer reaches 64° without even looking up from my work. My faithful field cricket starts his first scrapy tuning up almost exactly at that point every day. At 66° he is going "full organ" and I remove my coat and cap.

As the room becomes still warmer, it seems as though he were using a sustaining pedal. His notes, instead of each ending as he begins another, seem to persist and collect and pile up till the place is crammed to burst-

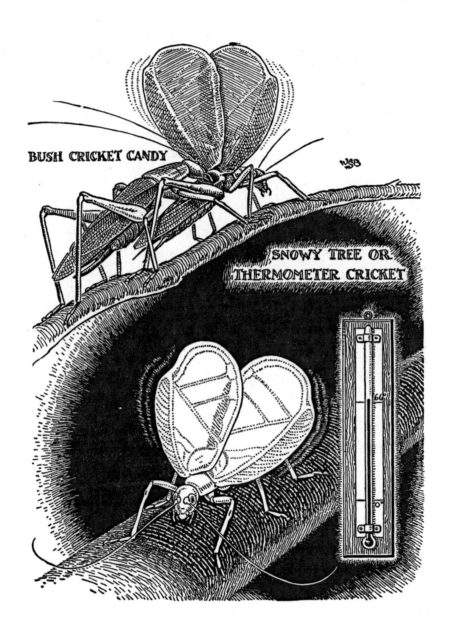

BUSH CRICKET CANDY

WSB

SNOWY TREE OR
THERMOMETER CRICKET

ing with them. Then if the day is coming on fair and sunny, I put the cage outdoors and try to collect my wits once more.

There are other smaller kinds of field crickets, but this kind, partly because of its large size—the body alone is one inch long—makes a charming pet. Crickets are kept as pets in various parts of the world, especially in Asia. People take them along and hang their cages in the trees to sing for them at picnics. In the Dutch East Indies the natives bet on cricket fights. Two males meet between their respective bamboo boxes. The one that pushes or chases the other back into his box first wins the bout. Seldom do the contestants really harm each other.

But there is no female present at such fights to egg the battlers on. My field cricket has a big black beautiful wife. One day, just to see how he would act, I put another male into the cage. Instantly he flew into a rage and rushed at the intruder. Fiddling furiously, jaws agape, he came close to the other male, holding fast to the floor with all his claws, but tensing all his leg muscles so that he swayed in angry jerks forward and back and from side to side. He became a veritable jitterbug, dancing all over without moving out of his tracks.

Almost as though embarrassed by the scene, and certainly bothered by such a cricket cursing, the new-comer kept moving away, only to be followed and threatened by the furious war dance again and again. Things quieted down after a while, but the irate husband was actually anything but peaceful in his heart. Though I was not a witness, he must have fought and killed his hated rival one dark night, for the following morning I found only the latter half of that unhappy insect lying on the cage floor amongst other edibles. For it was also evident that the husband and his wife had had a supper after the battle.

Though very jealous of possible attentions to his wife, my cricket has shown a peculiar interest in another female insect, not a cricket. There was a pair of red-legged locusts in the cage for some time, and he often dashed threateningly at the male grasshopper, or walked up and put his forehead against the grass-hopper's forehead and pushed him backward like a butting bull. At other times he simply shouldered him out of the way. But he always sidled gently up to the female grasshopper, edging in as close as he could, standing then beside her, playing his feelers over her and giving short slight chirps.

Once he placed his forehead against hers and once

against a slant-faced locust female's, but unlike his treatment of the male red-leg, he didn't push them around, just stood there apparently gazing into their glassy compound eyes. He inspects every grasshopper I introduce into the cage and seems to delight in tickling them with his feelers till they jump, while always walking well around their powerful hind legs out of the range of a backward kick.

I keep writing "evidently, apparently, as though," because I don't really know what prompts him to do some of the things he does. But I can't help wondering what sort of ideas are busy in his brain. For more than any other insect I have ever watched, yes, even more than ants, he seems to think. Ants often appear to think a lot about the work in hand, the routine daily toil. But this cricket acts like a free adventurer who goes about with an open mind, taking his fun where he finds it and having himself quite a time. Besides a set of strong feelings, he seems to have a very lively curiosity and some ability to satisfy it. When his wife had frantically dug a depression in the dirt and was sinking her long needle egg-placer deeply into the bottom of it, he stood by, touching her with his feelers, seemingly as interested as a human bystander watching someone using a pneumatic drill. Maybe he didn't understand what was taking place at all, but I'll wager he knew as much about it as some people do who watch men work with modern machinery.

He would go away and come back to stand chirping rather softly, maybe not sympathetically, perhaps just speculatively. When she finally finished her work and crawled up the wall, he stepped into the dirt box, wings raised as if to fiddle. But he didn't fiddle and yet he kept his wings up as though forgetting to lower them, so interested did he become in the dirt where she had been. Perhaps he was only interested in the scent of the slight amount of glue she left in the ground. It would be humanizing an insect to claim that he was aware that he had become a father, or that knowing this would matter to him. And yet, who knows? My brain is too different from his for me ever to know just what was in his mind. After a few moments he followed his wife up the wall and began befiddling her very gaily.

He appeared to take account of his wife's activities and act accordingly on another occasion. They were eating on the opposite ends of a section of green string bean pod as it lay upon the floor. Presently his wife extracted a small bean from the pod and carried it quickly into her sleeping box to eat. Immediately he hurried after and put his head in her door. She backed him out. Twice more he tried. The third time she emerged minus any sign of the bean and walked away. In he scurried and stayed for some time. I couldn't see him but it seemed certain that he was either enjoying a portion she had left or looking long, if futilely, for what she didn't leave.

These crickets don't spit when you pick them up. They are neat and tidy, sprucing up several times a day and doubtless during the night as well. Feelers are treated as katydids treat theirs. The sides of the body are rubbed with the hind legs moving from front to back. The two tail feelers are cleaned thus also. The chest is scraped by walking with it held against the floor, "chin" up, the underside of the abdomen being dragged the same way afterward. By throwing the hind leg way forward it can be licked from knee to end claws. And a surprising portion of the wings can be reached with the mouth by bringing them forward and laying the ends on the floor, one at a time.

Common from Canada to Patagonia, this big black cricket is not the kind Dickens wrote about in England. But it is likewise a very cheerful cricket to have on the hearth, unless it has only recently acquired

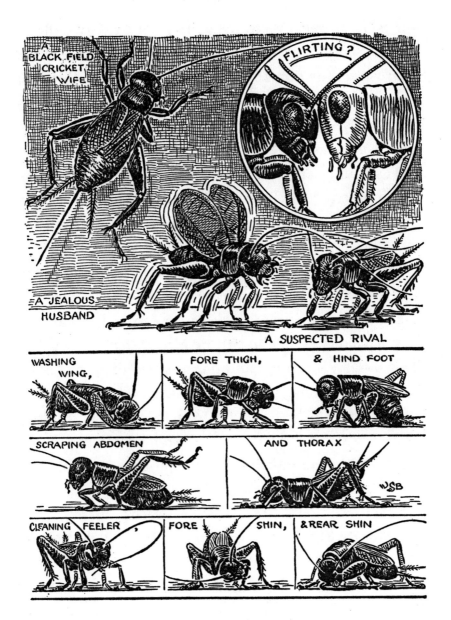

wings, its musical instrument. In such a case its efforts will be scrapy and of very poor tone at first, as is too true as well of human novices on the violin. But in a few days the tone and volume will have improved tremendously, and you can enjoy the truly cheerful quality it has taken on. Coming out from behind the woodbox as your cricket always will in the evening, it walks fiddling across the floor, almost as unafraid of you as the dog drowsing before the fire, secure in your friendship.

Friendship for crickets ends when too many enter our homes. Dickens wrote of a hearth that had one cricket. But sometimes they increase so in the walls of English houses that a person can scarcely sleep for their nightly chirping, and has a battle royal on his or her hands keeping them out of the food and furnishings. They can be as bad a pest as their cousins the roaches, except that no horrid aroma collects where they have been, and they do "sing" cheerfully, if too much at times.

When our field crickets come indoors in numbers, they forget the hearth and roam all over the house, getting into the food if they can and eating holes in carpets and curtains and everything made of cloth. So on the whole it is better that they stay in the fields and use their own burrows and go on eating grass and such good food.

Field crickets use burrows for the first half of the summer, living alone or at most in pairs. Later they

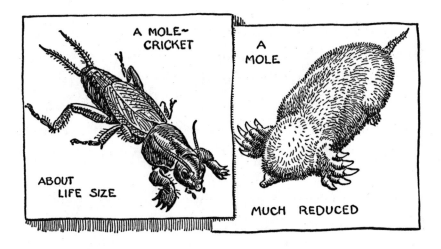

A MOLE-CRICKET

ABOUT LIFE SIZE

A MOLE

MUCH REDUCED

become very socially inclined and, except when they go in for wholesale house invasion, congregate in large numbers under the rubble of the fields and the rubbish of town dumps and such cranny-providing places. Frost ends their social season and most of their lives.

Whereas field crickets dig their temporary burrows with ordinary footgear, mole crickets are especially equipped for a life lived mostly underground and make themselves galleries as good as those of the much praised ant. It is believed that in these excellent quarters they live for more than just one season. Their eggs are laid in chambers which open on the galleries and since no drilling egg-placer is needed to get them underground, mole crickets do not have them.

All the important digging is done with apparatus at the other end. Here, as with their mammal namesake, is a remarkable development of the thorax, forelegs, and feet for gouging a passage through the earth by a sort of breast stroke motion. With this powerful equipment the mole cricket fairly swims along beneath the surface of the ground, humping it up as it goes very much as does the mole itself.

With strong projecting jaws it snips off roots that stretch across its course, and if the course happens to be through a garden, that is just too bad for the gardener. Its feelers are very stunted, as befits an insect of its habits. But the two tail-like members at its latter end are extra large and sensitive. They are useful as feelers when the mole cricket wants to back through the darkness of its diggings.

A good thing, from a gardener's point of view, is the fact that mole crickets prefer soil that is generally too damp for gardening. They are most common near swamps and ponds. Here, unseen, fiddling from just within their burrow openings, they are supposed by most human hearers to be peeping frogs.

And here we must leave the crickets to consider, for a little space, certain unwelcome comrades of life on shipboard and in town.

8

THE ROACHES

IT IS easy enough to give the grasshopper his due. One gladly says a good word for the katydid. And the cricket is a creature to be almost fond of out-of-doors, and to enjoy even more indoors if it is a blessing that comes singly. But just one cockroach is too many to delight us in our homes.

For no matter how often the cockroach cleans its feet and feelers, we may be reasonably sure that before it crawled into the cellar and came sneaking up through a thin crack between the water-pipes and floor it was making merry in some vile garbage dump or gutter. And now it wants the privilege of promenading on the pantry shelves and feasting in the cookie jar when darkness falls. Turn on the light and the thieving villain flees, drooling in its fear a brown saliva, the horrid scent of which remains, the calling card of a most unwelcome visitor.

Driven from the kitchen, it will go to the study perhaps, and gnaw the bindings of your books to get at the glue. Scrunching its flattest it will even devour the paste that holds the paper to the wall. Liking water-

colors though not appreciating art, it will eat the colors from your pictures and from your unclosed painting box.

The cockroach frequently does wash its feet; though, bathed in its own unsavory saliva, they can be clean only from its point of view and not from ours. Yet we can take advantage of its spruce-up habit to rid the house of its unlovely presence. If we scatter poisonous powders in the cracks where it crawls, some will collect on its feet. When next they are washed, enough poison will get into its mouth to kill it.

Splendid! But there are always others where it came from and so, in localities where cockroaches are common, defense against them must be continuous. Eternal vigilance is the price of purity, as it is of almost anything we cherish. Yet unless all help in the defense, some who have been the "have-nots" will become the "haves" and vice versa.

When a New York restaurant attacked its pest of roaches with poison chemicals, many were seen to leave by the front door, walk past six feet of masonry, and enter the restaurant next door with all the people. Of course, Old Mother Nature cared just as much for those roaches as for the customers. It wouldn't have mattered to her which fared the better, the insects or the humans. That was something for the restaurant men to worry about, especially the one who wasn't fumigating.

Despite our strong dislike for roaches, we must admire their power to persist. With no end of insect, reptile, bird, and mammal enemies after them for millions of years, and with every human hand against them since caves became mankind's first stationary homes, they still are with us in far too thriving a condition. Wherever we have stores of food, sooner or later they are likely to turn up.

Starting in the tropics, they have gone aboard ships in cargoes of provisions and thus traveled to and transplanted themselves in every land where people provide the food and warmth they want. Slaughterhouses, breweries, restaurants, and home kitchens are especially to their liking. And like those other undesirable aliens, the rats, they make a good thing of a life at sea. I used to gaze with horror at hordes of roaches that lived in the warm furnace room and dined in the steamy kitchen of a certain boarding school. But after I grew up and went to sea, I found that they were nothing as compared with the roaches which, given half a chance, will thrive on ships, especially in warm climates.

A sea-cook friend of mine, working on a small West Indies schooner, sometimes had a chance while the dough was rising to take a nap. But if he lay down for only a few minutes, often as not he would wake with his face smarting terribly. On looking into a mirror he found that roaches, eating the galley grease from his face, had taken the outer layer of his hide as well. And each night they chewed the calluses on the bare feet of sleeping members of the crew. Things get pretty bad on vessels whose owners do not fumigate.

Always lurking where there is unfailing warmth, roaches can lay their eggs the year around, and do.

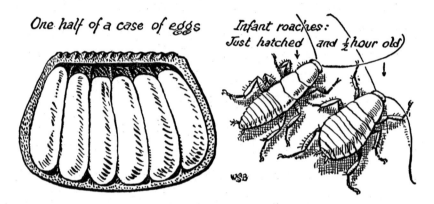

One half of a case of eggs   Infant roaches: Just hatched and ½ hour old

But, unlike most rapid multipliers of the insect world, roaches have long lives, several years perhaps, so that their hatch rate greatly exceeds their death rate. Thus their population increases enormously unless something drastic is done about it.

There are more than a thousand different kinds of roaches, mostly brown or blackish, though there are green or striped or spotted kinds too. Some have eggs that hatch just before being laid so that the young appear to be born. But most kinds of cockroach mothers carry for a time what looks like a bulging handbag, actually a horny egg case or capsule attached to the end of the body. In it are between one and two dozen eggs.

When the time is ripe, she leaves this portable incubator in some warm, damp, cozy crevice where the young ones will get on nicely when they hatch. On emerging from the eggs, they find themselves facing the "zipper" edge of the case with little chance of facing any other way so closely are they packed, each in its own groove. The only way to go is forward, in which they are assisted by small backward-pointing spines projecting from their hatching-skins. Probably all that is needed to break the cement that seals the side of the case they are pointed toward is a little push, perhaps from several at the same time. Some say that the first thing they do is drool, which is one of the first things they do as adults when in a tight spot. Their saliva is supposed to melt the cement. But this has not been proved, as far as I can find out. Personally I have never been inside a cockroach capsule just as the babies were about to break out of it. But it does open a wee mite, maybe a sixteenth of an inch or less, and out they come, leaving their hatching-skins behind as they crawl through their first thin crack. Thereafter the wide world is theirs, with its limitless scavenging possibilities.

Most roaches have wings, though the females of some kinds aren't so provided. Roaches living always

indoors in cooler climates seldom use their wings, except as slippery surfaces to aid in slithering through the shallowest cracks, aided also by great ability to flatten their bodies. But in the tropics, where some are four inches long, they fly at night, entering lighted houses and often pursued by bats. Several kinds of tropical roaches belong to the great insect orchestra.

Some, by rubbing one part of the thorax on another part or on the bases of their upper wings, make a faint little noise, sometimes known as drumming. And in Madagascar, a large kind of roach can make a grunting sound by suddenly forcing air out through the breathing holes along its sides. What the roaches hear with is not known; perhaps part of their long antennae, and possibly the hairs on their legs and bodies, are sensitive to sounds.

The ant in Aesop's fable may have turned the grasshopper from its door. But some tropical parasol ants actually invite the company of certain stunted cousins of the grasshopper, a tiny kind of cockroach, into their homes. These roaches love the oils exuded from the armor of the ants, and the ants love to be licked. So they go through their galleries with minute roaches riding pick-a-back. On the other hand, another kind of ant kills bigger roaches and carries them home for food, if it finds them feeding in the jungle flowers. This is a good thing for orchids, the roaches having the habit of eating the roots of these gorgeous air plants.

The Mexicans, whose language is so beautiful, don't like roaches any better than the rest of us. But they have a song about them which you may have heard. How much more musical "Cucaracha" sounds! Only in Spanish can we find the heart to sing of the craven cockroach.

It rightly has a hang-dog look, its chin forever on its chest, its eyes cast down. Its thorax all but covers

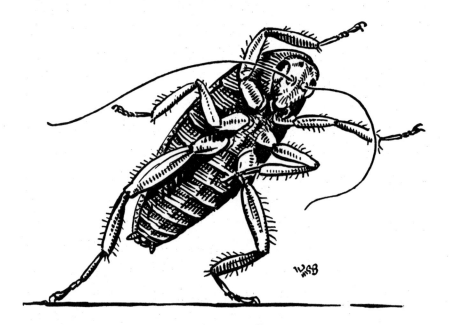

its head, like a cringing man with hat pulled down, collar turned up, and shoulders raised to fend off the crushing blow he perpetually expects. We cannot even feel enthusiasm for the wretched roaches by reminding ourselves that their ancestors were also ancestors of termites, whose great insect nations, with their workers, soldiers, queens, and even kings, rival those in the wonder world of ants. For are not termites our tormentors too, invading and destroying our homes?

The Oriental roach, which is common in the Occident as well, is said to prey on bed-bugs. The horrific-looking centipede in turn devours roaches. But none of these indoor creatures can be considered with a happy heart. Each is about as undesirable as the ones it preys upon. The cure is hardly better than the misery.

Shall we go outdoors again and get a breath of good fresh air, with walking-sticks?

9

WALKING-STICKS

NOW a walking-stick walking by itself would be a vision unbelievable. Seeing a cane tripping nimbly up the street, with no human hand to hold it, would make us wonder if we were dreaming or just going crazy. If only a little three inch stick lying by a bush should rise an inch from the ground supported by its tiny twigs, move toward the bush, climb it, and place itself back on the branch from which it fell, we would have the same inability to believe our eyes.

Yet this, or some scene like it, is what we seem to witness the first time we see a stick-insect, or walking-stick. Because, until it moves, we are almost certain not to notice it at all. Not only does it look exactly like the real twigs on the branch in shape, size, and color, but it acts like one for hours at a time during daylight. Pressing against the branch with its latter end and leaning out a little with the other, it extends its forelegs and feelers straight before it, appearing thus to taper off in true twig style.

The forelegs are curved at the end next the body to fit snugly around the very small head so that they

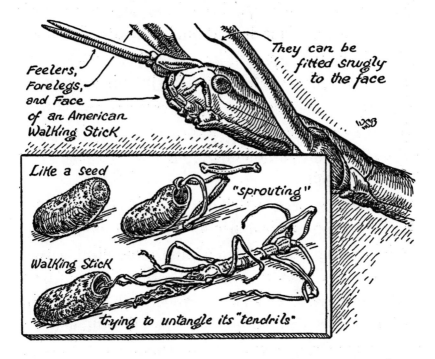

Feelers, Forelegs, and Face of an American Walking Stick

They can be fitted snugly to the face

Like a seed

"sprouting"

Walking Stick

trying to untangle its "tendrils"

meet in front of the face and continue outward together. The face seems scarcely big enough for all its features, the mouth with its many parts (lips, tongue, tasting feelers, and jaws), plus the forehead feelers and the compound eyes. Yet everything is there and without destroying the wondrous twiggy outline of

119

the walking-stick disguise.

Even before this insect hatches it is already imitating plants. There is something plant-like in the very way the eggs are laid. For the female in the tree lets her eggs drop hit-or-miss, with no more concern for their future than a plant has, dropping seeds. The eggs themselves look so much like seeds that trained botanists have collected them by mistake. Since walking-sticks are numerous only every other year, it is believed that the eggs, like certain seeds, lie under the leaves for two winters before bursting open to free new lives into the world.

In the very act of hatching, the baby stick-insect is first like a sprout, then a tangled tendril, and finally, straightening out its kinks and crumples, a twig colored green or brown in the best of twig traditions.

If, before the insect is full grown, it loses one of its members, it can sprout another where the old one was, a power more common in plants than animals. Starting late, the new leg will not have time to get as large as the others before the last molt ends all growing. It will be smaller and may be bent somewhat, but better than an empty socket on the insect's side.

In spite of all this marvelous mimicry, the walking-stick still fails to feel entirely secure, and tries one more trick when considering itself in danger. If a bird alights, shaking the branch a trifle where the walking-stick is fastened, it "breaks off" and falls to the ground just as a dead and brittle twig would do. Rapping the branches of trees in a big walking-stick year brings hundreds of them down, sounding as they hit the rubbish of the forest floor like a shower of hail. With eggs falling from countless females, a similar sound is created.

There have been walking-stick plagues in the eastern half of this country when the twigs of oak, chestnut, and maple trees were stripped as bare of leaves as the walking-sticks themselves. On the other hand, certain intimate tropical relatives of walking-sticks mimic leaves instead of twigs. The bodies, wings, and legs of walking-leaves or leaf insects are ironed out flat in perfect pale green leaf designs. It must be equally astonishing to see a cluster of leaves climbing about as to watch a walking-stick on the move.

A large walking-stick of New Guinea is heavy-set and very rough and spiny like the bark of the trees it prefers to feed upon. It is six inches long. But the largest walking-stick, and perhaps the largest of all insects, is an African walking-stick with a ten and one-half inch body, a total length of sixteen inches with

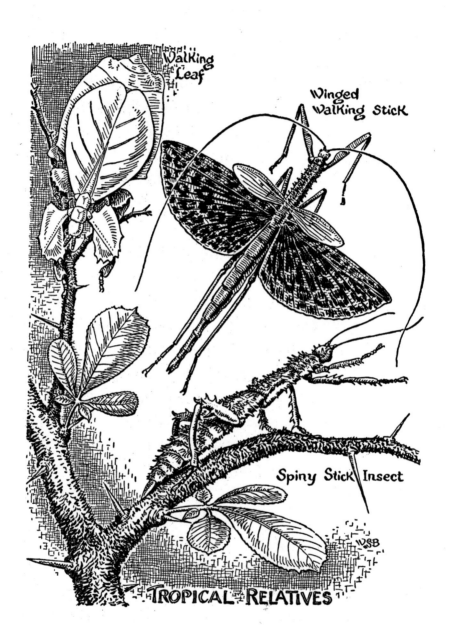

Walking Leaf

Winged Walking Stick

Spiny Stick Insect

TROPICAL RELATIVES

forelegs extended, and a wingspread of nine inches
from tip to tip. Another kind, eight inches long, found
in Brazil, is called the stinking-stick insect because, as
a final defense, it will spray an acrid stinging liquid at
its enemies from openings on the sides of its thorax.
This smells so horribly that the hungry enemy loses all
appetite and is only too glad to get away from there.
Several kinds of walking-sticks in our southern states
can defend themselves thus also, one squirting a milky
spray for a foot and a half or more that burns your
skin and painfully stings your eyes. Such walking-
sticks are the skunks of the insect world.

Our three-inch northern walking-sticks have no
wings, but many tropical kinds have very good ones
which, like those of our band-winged locusts, only dis-
play their beauty when the insects fly.

There remains only one branch more of the grasshopper's family tree. Its members are those terrible
relatives which, while posing so piously, live entirely
by murder, not being safe even from each other.

10

THE PRAYING MANTISES

PRAYING MANTISES they are called, but if they were billed as a vaudeville troupe in life's continuous performance they would come on as the Murdering Mantises, the Mangling Maniacs, or maybe the Horrible Hypocrites.

Whoever named them thought he saw in their up-raised forelegs the attitude of prayer. Some have called them soothsayers, which means truthtellers, because of this pious posture. But to tell the truth, for what may they be praying? Are they asking forgiveness for their many murders and at the same time petitioning for more victims? That would be hypocritical enough. For the truth is that the forelegs are not raised to pray, but to prey.

Never using these hook- and dagger-studded limbs for walking, the mantis holds them folded restfully but always ready. With weapons thus concealed, it may stealthily stalk its victim or play a waiting game,

124

moving nothing but its head, which can be turned on the long, neck-like thorax to look on all sides and even behind, an act no other insect can perform. With great black compound eyes held steadily on the prey until

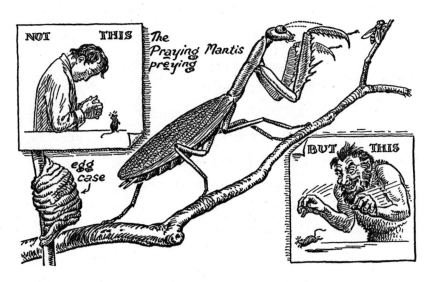

it comes into snatching range, it suddenly springs its terrible trap. The awful arms shoot out and grapple the victim, pinning it in a score of places and pulling it to the ever hungry mouth of the mantis.

Most frequently the prey is some other insect, anything from mosquitoes up to its own jumping relatives, the grasshoppers and katydids. It quickly bites off the heads of these kickers to stop their disturbing struggles and make the eating easier.

Caterpillars are consumed entirely, but the harder portions of jointed insects are discarded. Spiders, though possessing poison fangs, are very much afraid of mantises and are liable to lose their lives when they do attempt to tangle with them. The mantises of Europe and Asia and of our southern states, and most of those of tropical America, are green or brown. But some of the tropical kinds wear the hues of orchids, in which they lurk to trap the other insects visiting these gorgeous flowers. Sometimes even small birds, also seeking insects there, are captured and devoured.

Yet a small mouse has been seen to box with a mantis, making swift swipes and receiving some scratches as the insect struck back, but finally going into a clinch and killing it with a bite back of the head. And the mantis is harmless to humans. In fact it is very helpful to us, destroying a multitude of insects which do damage to our crops.

But one mantis can be very harmful to another. The female is very likely to eat the slightly smaller male when the mating is over. Poor creature, at least he helps a little to nourish the eggs that she will lay. She places as many as one hundred of them on some twig, surrounded by a hardening froth of glue.

Sometimes a certain kind of wasp also lays in the

froth before it sets, and the wasp grubs grow by eating the mantis' eggs. There is a kind of fly which pierces the hardened froth with a sting-like egg-placer, and its maggots fatten as the wasp grubs do. Ants eat infant mantises as they hatch, or growing mantises if they find them eating aphids, the ants' nectar cows. They kill the poachers and carry them off to store for food. Birds and monkeys also help themselves to young and growing mantises.

But though it has some enemies to fear, the mature mantis remains among the most terrible of insect hobgoblins. The Devil's Race Horse is another name for it, but in the insect world it rather plays the part of the very Old Boy himself.

Cannot you hear the fiendish laughter as the Arch Mantis of all mantises says to a trembling Aesop,

"You're a fabulating sissy! *I'm* the one who can put a grasshopper in its place!"

But about praying mantises, as with grasshoppers and ants, it's very probable that poor old Aesop never really knew.

Printed in the United States
125182LV00002B/11-20/P

9 780865 346901